SharePoint 2013 Solution Series Volumes 1-5

Volume 1

How To Create a WCF Web Service in SharePoint 2013

STEVEN MANN

How To Create a WCF Web Service in SharePoint 2013

Copyright © 2013 by Steven Mann

Trademarks

Screenshots of Microsoft Products and Services

Warning and Disclaimer

Introduction

Many times you need to access SharePoint data from a web service. This could be for custom web parts, InfoPath Forms, BCS purposes, etc. When you need to access Share-Point data (e.g. list items, document information, etc.), the best method in SharePoint 2013 is to create a custom WCF web service that lives on your SharePoint farm. This Kindle e-book steps you through the process of generating a custom WCF web service that is deployed to SharePoint itself.

Reference links and source code is available on www.stevethemanmann.com:

SteveMann's Path   **S**> SharePoint   **O** Office

Discussions on technology related to collaboration with SharePoint and InfoPath along with other cool and possibly geeky stuff.

Blog   Available Speaking Topics   Resource Links and Source Code

Step 1 - Visual Studio 2012 Project

The first step is to open up Visual Studio 2012 in a SharePoint development environment and create a new project using the SharePoint Empty Project template:

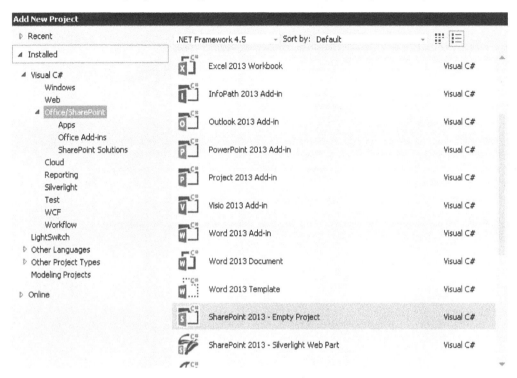

Specify the SharePoint URL for debugging purposes and select Deploy as a farm solution:

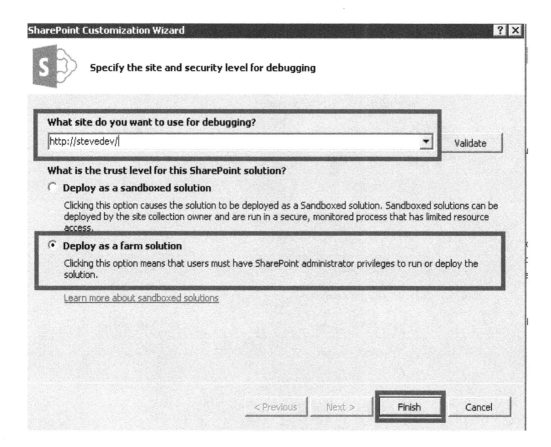

Click Finish.

Step 2 - Leverage the WCF Project Template

Your SharePoint project needs the WCF service components. It is easier to have them generated from a WCF project and copy them into your SharePoint WCF project. Therefore, add a new project to your solution but this time select WCF Service Library:

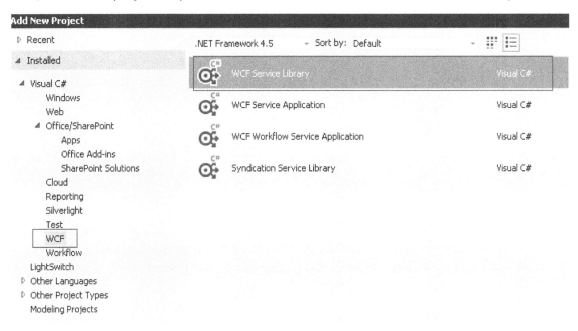

Step 3 - Copy the Service Classes to Your SharePoint WCF Project

Copy the IService1.cs and Service1.cs files that were generated in the WcfServiceLibrary project into your SharePoint WCF project:

You can either use Copy/Paste or select the classes and drag them up to your SharePoint WCF project.

Once these files have been copied into your SharePoint WCF project, you may remove the WCF Service Library project from your solution:

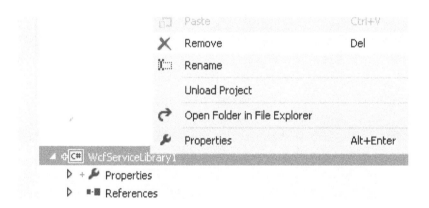

Step 4 - Add References to Your SharePoint WCF Project

You need to add the following references to your SharePoint WCF project:

System.Runtime.Serialization

System.ServiceModel

System.ServiceModel.Web

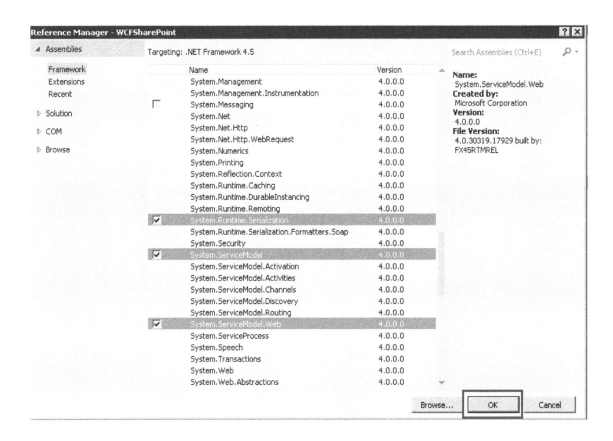

When you create an Empty SharePoint project, the Microsoft.SharePoint and Microsoft.SharePoint.Client.ServerRuntime references are already in place. You no longer need to add these as you may have had done in previous versions of Visual Studio and/or SharePoint.

Step 5 - Define your Service and Data Contracts in the Service Interface

In your interface file (IService1.cs), remove the current operation contracts and define your own for your WCF service.

```
namespace WcfServiceLibrary1
{
    // NOTE: You can use the "Rename" command on the "Refactor" menu to change the in
    [ServiceContract]
    public interface IService1
    {
        [OperationContract]
        string GetData(int value);

        [OperationContract]
        CompositeType GetDataUsingDataContract(CompositeType composite);

        // TODO: Add your service operations here
    }
}
```

For example purposes, I needed to create a WCF Service for BCS and Search which requires a ReadItem method and a ReadList method. Therefore, in my ServiceContract, I created two OperationContracts:

```
[ServiceContract]
public interface IEventsService
{

    [OperationContract]
    EventItem ReadItem(string id);

    [OperationContract]
    List<EventItem> ReadList();

}
```

The implementation of these methods will read list items in a SharePoint Calendar list and return the data within an object. In my example, the object is an EventItem which is a custom class. Therefore, in my DataContract, I needed to define the EventItem class:

```csharp
// Use a data contract as illustrated in the sample bel
[DataContract]
public class EventItem : IComparable, IComparer
{
    private string _eventID;
    [DataMember]
    public string EventID
    {
        get { return _eventID; }
        set { _eventID = value; }
    }



    private string _URL;
    [DataMember]
    public string URL
    {
        get { return _URL; }
        set { _URL = value; }
    }

    private string _title;
    [DataMember]
    public string Title
    {
        get { return _title; }
        set { _title = value; }
    }

    private string _body;
    [DataMember]
    public string Body
    {
        get { return _body; }
        set { _body = value; }
    }
}
```

Notice each property of my class is described as a DataMember using the [DataMember] attribute.

Step 6 - Prep the Service Class

The service class (Service1.cs) implements the operations that you defined in the interface, however, there are some preparations that need to be performed first.

At the top of the Service1.cs class file, add the following using statements:

using Microsoft.SharePoint;

using Microsoft.SharePoint.Client.Services;

using System.ServiceModel.Activation;

You may copy and paste this from stevethemanmann.com

```
using Microsoft.SharePoint;
using Microsoft.SharePoint.Client.Services;
using System;
using System.Collections.Generic;
using System.Diagnostics;
using System.Linq;
using System.Runtime.Serialization;
using System.ServiceModel;
using System.ServiceModel.Activation;
using System.ServiceModel.Web;
using System.Text;
```

Add the following attributes your service class:

[BasicHttpBindingServiceMetadataExchangeEndpointAttribute]

[AspNetCompatibilityRequirements(RequirementsMode = AspNetCompatibilityRequirementsMode.Required)]

You may copy and paste this from stevethemanmann.com

```
[BasicHttpBindingServiceMetadataExchangeEndpointAttribute]
[AspNetCompatibilityRequirements(RequirementsMode = AspNetCompatibilityRequirementsMode.Required)]
public class EventService : IEventsService
{
```

Step 7 - Implement the Service Methods

In your Service class, add the implementation of the methods that you previously defined within your service interface.

For my BCS example, I needed to implement a ReadItem method:

```
public class EventService : IEventsService
{

    public EventItem ReadItem(string id)
    {

        .....
        return eventItem;

    }
}
```

I also needed to implement a ReadList method:

```
public List<EventItem> ReadList()
{

    List<EventItem> eventItems = new List<EventItem>();

    .....
    return eventItems;

}
```

Step 8 - Create the SharePoint Service Registration File

The moving parts of the WCF service are now completed, however, in order for the service to be deployed and workable in SharePoint, the .svc file needs to be created. The .svc file contains the WCF service information as well as the referenced assembly (.dll) that is generated when you build the solution. The assembly information is added into the registration file upon the build and deployment of your SharePoint WCF Service.

Web services in SharePoint live in the ISAPI folder on each web-front-end and are referenced using /_vti_bin/ within a SharePoint URL. Therefore, you must create an ISAPI folder in your project and then create the registration file within the ISAPI folder.

Right-click your SharePoint WCF project and select Add. Then select SharePoint Mapped folder...

The Add SharePoint Mapped Folder dialog appears.

In the Add SharePoint Mapped Folder dialog select ISAPI and click OK:

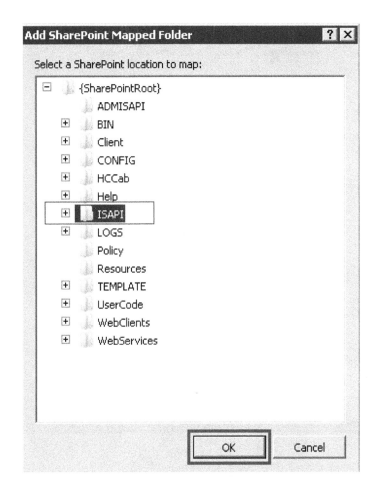

The ISAPI folder is added to your project.

Next, you need to create the registration file within the ISAPI folder. Therefore, right-click the ISAPI folder in your project and select Add. Select New Item...

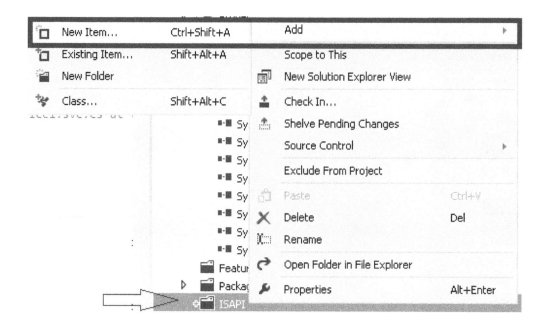

From the General section, select Text File and name your file with a .svc extension. Click Add:

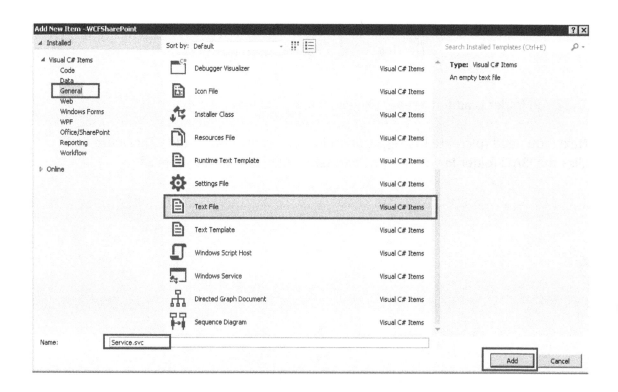

Open the Service.svc file that was created and add the following code:

```
<%@ServiceHost Language="C#" Debug="true"
    Service="WcfService.ServiceName, $SharePoint.Project.AssemblyFullName$"
    Factory="Microsoft.SharePoint.Client.Services.MultipleBaseAddressBasicHttpBindingServiceHostFactory,
Microsoft.SharePoint.Client.ServerRuntime, Version=15.0.0.0, Culture=neutral,
PublicKeyToken=71e9bce111e9429c" %>
```

You may copy and paste this from stevethemanmann.com

```
<%@ServiceHost Language="C#" Debug="true"
    Service="WcfService.ServiceName, $SharePoint.Project.AssemblyFullName$"
    Factory="Microsoft.SharePoint.Client.Services.MultipleBaseAddressBasicHttpBindingServiceHostFactory, Microsoft.SharePoi
```

Save the file changes.

Step 9 - Activate Token Replacements for Service Files

The code that you pasted into the .svc file contains the assembly full name token ($SharePoint.Project.AssemblyFullName$). Visual Studio replaces this with the assembly from your project during build and deployment. However, you must instruct Visual Studio to perform this in .svc files.

This requires a modification to the actual project file of your SharePoint WCF service. Since it is open in Visual Studio, first right-click your project and select Unload Project.

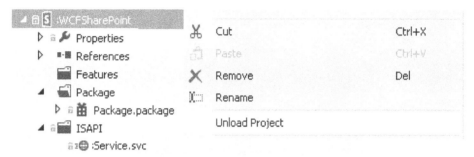

Now locate the project file from the file system and edit in a text editor (e.g. NotePad).

Add the following property tag to the project file within the <PropertyGroup> section:

<TokenReplacementFileExtensions>svc</TokenReplacementFileExtensions>

```
WCFSharePoint - Notepad
File  Edit  Format  View  Help
<?xml version="1.0" encoding="utf-8"?>
<Project ToolsVersion="4.0" DefaultTargets="Build" xmlns="http://schemas.microsoft.com/developer/msbuild/2003">
  <Import Project="$(MSBuildExtensionsPath)\$(MSBuildToolsVersion)\Microsoft.Common.props" Condition="Exists('$(MSBuildExten
  <PropertyGroup>
    <Configuration Condition=" '$(Configuration)' == '' ">Debug</Configuration>
    <Platform Condition=" '$(Platform)' == '' ">AnyCPU</Platform>
    <ProjectGuid>{3F89918B-A0B6-4B5B-B087-9E6F1FC487E1}</ProjectGuid>
    <OutputType>Library</OutputType>
    <AppDesignerFolder>Properties</AppDesignerFolder>
    <RootNamespace>FirmEventsWCFSharePoint</RootNamespace>
    <AssemblyName>FirmEventsWCFSharePoint</AssemblyName>
    <TargetFrameworkVersion>v4.5</TargetFrameworkVersion>
    <TargetOfficeVersion>15.0</TargetOfficeVersion>
    <FileAlignment>512</FileAlignment>
    <ProjectTypeGuids>{C1CDDADD-2546-481F-9697-4EA41081F2FC};{14822709-B5A1-4724-98CA-57A101D1B079};{FAE04EC0-301F-11D3-BF4B
    <SccProjectName>SAK</SccProjectName>
    <SccLocalPath>SAK</SccLocalPath>
    <SccAuxPath>SAK</SccAuxPath>
    <SccProvider>SAK</SccProvider>
    <TokenReplacementFileExtensions>svc</TokenReplacementFileExtensions>
  </PropertyGroup>
  <PropertyGroup Condition=" '$(Configuration)|$(Platform)' == 'Debug|AnyCPU' ">
    <DebugSymbols>true</DebugSymbols>
    <DebugType>full</DebugType>
    <Optimize>false</Optimize>
    <OutputPath>bin\Debug\</OutputPath>
    <DefineConstants>DEBUG;TRACE</DefineConstants>
    <ErrorReport>prompt</ErrorReport>
    <WarningLevel>4</WarningLevel>
    <UseVSHostingProcess>false</UseVSHostingProcess>
  </PropertyGroup>
  <PropertyGroup Condition=" '$(Configuration)|$(Platform)' == 'Release|AnyCPU' ">
    <DebugType>pdbonly</DebugType>
    <Optimize>true</Optimize>
    <OutputPath>bin\Release\</OutputPath>
```

Save the changes and Reload the project within Visual Studio:

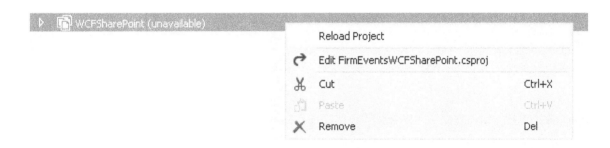

Step 10 - Deploy Your SharePoint WCF Service

Right-click your solution and select Deploy. Visual Studio builds your solution, generates an assembly, updates the .svc file, creates a WSP file for deployment to stage/production, and deploys your SharePoint WCF service to your development SharePoint environment.

Step 11 - Test Your SharePoint WCF in SharePoint

Once your solution has been deployed, you may access the WCF service in SharePoint using the SharePoint root URL along with the path to the service:

http://<<sharepoint root>>/_vti_bin/Service.svc

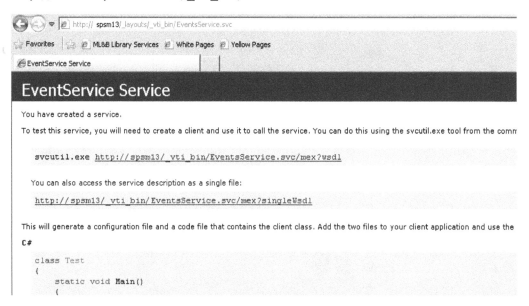

To fully test the service you need to call it from a client application or use the svcutil.exe tool to invoke the service methods to insure data is being returned.

Using Your WCF Service in BCS

When creating an external content type using a SharePoint WCF Service, you need to enter and select the proper selections. This section shows examples of these settings:

Service Metadata URL

http://<<sharepoint root>/_vti_bin/Service.svc/mex?wsdl

Metadata Connection Mode

WSDL

Service EndPoint URL

http://<<sharepoint root>>/_vti_bin/Service.svc

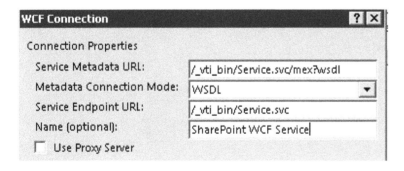

Conclusion

In just a handful of steps you can easily create a WCF Service in SharePoint that serves up SharePoint data. Using the WCF Service Library template as a guide and an empty SharePoint project, Visual Studio 2012 provides the tools and functionality to generate and deploy a SharePoint WCF service.

I hope you found this guide useful and informative. If you have any troubles or other questions, please send them to me at steve@stevethemanmann.com.

Volume 2

How To Integrate BCS with Search in SharePoint 2013

STEVEN MANN

How To Integrate BCS with Search in SharePoint 2013

Copyright © 2013 by Steven Mann

Trademarks

Screenshots of Microsoft Products and Services

Warning and Disclaimer

Introduction

This guide steps you through the process of incorporating external data into SharePoint 2013 Search by leveraging Business Data Connectivity Services (BCS). It provides an end-to-end solution that integrates product data from a SQL Server database into SharePoint by using external content types. Creating a new search vertical as well as customizing the display and hover panels of the business data search results is also covered.

Reference links and source code are available on www.stevethemanmann.com:

Step 1: Prepare the Data Source

The scenario and sample data for this guide uses Product information from the AdventureWorks2012 sample database in SQL Server.

The first step is to create your read list and read item procedures.

Create a stored procedure that returns all of the information you want to search and make sure all rows are returned:

```sql
CREATE PROCEDURE GetAllProductsForBCS
AS
BEGIN
    -- SET NOCOUNT ON added to prevent extra result sets from
    -- interfering with SELECT statements.
    SET NOCOUNT ON;

    -- Insert statements for procedure here
    SELECT
        p.ProductID,
        p.ProductNumber,
        p.Name AS ProductName,
        p.Class AS ProductClass,
        p.Color AS ProductColor,
        p.ProductLine,
        p.ListPrice AS ProductListPrice,
        pc.Name AS ProductCategory,
        psc.Name AS ProductSubCategory,
        pm.Name AS ProductModel,
        pd.Description as ProductDescription
    FROM Production.Product p
```

100 % ▾ ‹

Results | Messages

	ProductID	ProductNumber	ProductName	ProductClass	ProductColor	ProductLine	ProductListPrice	ProductCategory	ProductSubCategory	ProductModel	ProductDescription
1	994	BB-7421	LL Bottom Bracket	L	NULL	NULL	53.99	Components	Bottom Brackets	LL Bottom Bracket	Chromoly steel.
2	995	BB-8107	ML Bottom Bracket	M	NULL	NULL	101.24	Components	Bottom Brackets	ML Bottom Bracket	Aluminum alloy cups; large d
3	996	BB-9108	HL Bottom Bracket	H	NULL	NULL	121.49	Components	Bottom Brackets	HL Bottom Bracket	Aluminum alloy cups and a h
4	984	BK-M18S-40	Mountain-500 Silver, 40	L	Silver	M	564.99	Bikes	Mountain Bikes	Mountain-500	Suitable for any type of riding
5	985	BK-M18S-42	Mountain-500 Silver, 42	L	Silver	M	564.99	Bikes	Mountain Bikes	Mountain-500	Suitable for any type of riding
6	986	BK-M18S-44	Mountain-500 Silver, 44	L	Silver	M	564.99	Bikes	Mountain Bikes	Mountain-500	Suitable for any type of riding
7	987	BK-M18S-48	Mountain-500 Silver, 48	L	Silver	M	564.99	Bikes	Mountain Bikes	Mountain-500	Suitable for any type of riding
8	988	BK-M18S-52	Mountain-500 Silver, 52	L	Silver	M	564.99	Bikes	Mountain Bikes	Mountain-500	Suitable for any type of riding
9	989	BK-M18B-40	Mountain-500 Black, 40	L	Black	M	539.99	Bikes	Mountain Bikes	Mountain-500	Suitable for any type of riding
10	990	BK-M18B-42	Mountain-500 Black, 42	L	Black	M	539.99	Bikes	Mountain Bikes	Mountain-500	Suitable for any type of riding
11	991	BK-M18B-44	Mountain-500 Black, 44	L	Black	M	539.99	Bikes	Mountain Bikes	Mountain-500	Suitable for any type of riding
12	992	BK-M18B-48	Mountain-500 Black, 48	L	Black	M	539.99	Bikes	Mountain Bikes	Mountain-500	Suitable for any type of riding
13	993	BK-M18B-52	Mountain-500 Black, 52	L	Black	M	539.99	Bikes	Mountain Bikes	Mountain-500	Suitable for any type of riding
14	980	BK-M38S-38	Mountain-400-W Silver, 38	M	Silver	M	769.49	Bikes	Mountain Bikes	Mountain-400-W	This bike delivers a high-leve

I created a GetAllProductsForBCS stored procedure which returns the product information I need using several joins:

```sql
CREATE PROCEDURE GetAllProductsForBCS
AS
BEGIN
        -- SET NOCOUNT ON added to prevent extra result sets from
        -- interfering with SELECT statements.
        SET NOCOUNT ON;

    -- Insert statements for procedure here
        SELECT
                p.ProductID,
                p.ProductNumber,
                p.Name AS ProductName,
                p.Class AS ProductClass,
                p.Color AS ProductColor,
                p.ProductLine,
                p.ListPrice AS ProductListPrice,
                pc.Name AS ProductCategory,
                psc.Name AS ProductSubCategory,
                pm.Name AS ProductModel,
                pd.Description as ProductDescription
        FROM Production.Product p
                INNER JOIN Production.ProductSubcategory psc
                        ON psc.ProductSubcategoryID = p.ProductSubcategoryID
                INNER JOIN Production.ProductCategory pc
                        ON pc.ProductCategoryID = psc.ProductCategoryID
                INNER JOIN Production.ProductModel pm
                        on pm.ProductModelID = p.ProductModelID
                 INNER JOIN Production.ProductModelProductDescriptionCulture pmx
                        ON pm.ProductModelID = pmx.ProductModelID
                INNER JOIN Production.ProductDescription pd
                        ON pmx.ProductDescriptionID = pd.ProductDescriptionID
        WHERE pmx.CultureID='en'
```

This procedure is used to create a ReadList method in the External Content Type.

Create a stored procedure that returns the same information but only for a particular entity by using the ID as a parameter:

```sql
--exec GetProductByProductIDforBCS 995
CREATE PROCEDURE GetProductByProductIDforBCS (@ProductID INT)
AS
BEGIN
    -- SET NOCOUNT ON added to prevent extra result sets from
    -- interfering with SELECT statements.
    SET NOCOUNT ON;

    -- Insert statements for procedure here
    SELECT
        p.ProductID,
        p.ProductNumber,
        p.Name AS ProductName,
        p.Class AS ProductClass,
        p.Color AS ProductColor,
        p.ProductLine,
        p.ListPrice AS ProductListPrice,
        pc.Name AS ProductCategory,
        psc.Name AS ProductSubCategory,
        pm.Name AS ProductModel,
        pd.Description as ProductDescription
    FROM Production.Product p
        INNER JOIN Production.ProductSubcategory psc
            ON psc.ProductSubcategoryID = p.ProductSubcategoryID
        INNER JOIN Production.ProductCategory pc
            ON pc.ProductCategoryID = psc.ProductCategoryID
        INNER JOIN Production.ProductModel pm
            on pm.ProductModelID = p.ProductModelID
        INNER JOIN Production.ProductModelProductDescriptionCulture pmx
            ON pm.ProductModelID = pmx.ProductModelID
        INNER JOIN Production.ProductDescription pd
            ON pmx.ProductDescriptionID = pd.ProductDescriptionID
    WHERE p.ProductID = @ProductID
        AND pmx.CultureID='en'
```

100 %   <

Results Messages

ProductID	ProductNumber	ProductName	ProductClass	ProductColor	ProductLine	ProductListPrice	ProductCategory	ProductSubCategory	ProductModel	ProductDescription
1	995	BB-8107	ML Bottom Bracket	M	NULL	NULL	101.24	Components	Bottom Brackets	ML Bottom Bracket	Aluminum alloy cups; large diameter s

Make sure only 1 row is returned for a given identity.

I created a GetAllProductsForBCS stored procedure which returns the product information I need based on the passed in ProductID parameter:

```sql
CREATE PROCEDURE GetProductByProductIDForBCS (@ProductID INT)
AS
BEGIN
        -- SET NOCOUNT ON added to prevent extra result sets from
        -- interfering with SELECT statements.
        SET NOCOUNT ON;

    -- Insert statements for procedure here
        SELECT
                p.ProductID,
                p.ProductNumber,
                p.Name AS ProductName,
                p.Class AS ProductClass,
                p.Color AS ProductColor,
                p.ProductLine,
                p.ListPrice AS ProductListPrice,
                pc.Name AS ProductCategory,
                psc.Name AS ProductSubCategory,
                pm.Name AS ProductModel,
                pd.Description as ProductDescription
        FROM Production.Product p
                INNER JOIN Production.ProductSubcategory psc
                        ON psc.ProductSubcategoryID = p.ProductSubcategoryID
                INNER JOIN Production.ProductCategory pc
                        ON pc.ProductCategoryID = psc.ProductCategoryID
                INNER JOIN Production.ProductModel pm
                        on pm.ProductModelID = p.ProductModelID
                 INNER JOIN Production.ProductModelProductDescriptionCulture pmx
                        ON pm.ProductModelID = pmx.ProductModelID
                INNER JOIN Production.ProductDescription pd
                        ON pmx.ProductDescriptionID = pd.ProductDescriptionID
        WHERE p.ProductID = @ProductID
                AND pmx.CultureID='en'
```

This procedure is used to create a ReadItem method in the External Content Type. The SELECT statement here should be exactly the same as the SELECT in the ReadList. The only difference here is that additional WHERE condition for the passed in @ProductID.

Step 2: Add Credentials to the Secure Store Service

In order for the External Content Type to be created and BCS to access your external data source, the data source credentials need to be stored. The Secure Store Service in SharePoint allows you to store credentials. For this scenario, a SQL database account was created named "AWDBAccount". Therefore an entry in the Secure Store Service needs to be added for SQL Authentication.

Navigate to Central Administration and click on Manage Service Applications under the Application Management section:

Click on the Secure Store Service application link:

Search Administration Web Service for Search Service Application

Search Service Application

    Search Service Application Proxy

Secure Store Service

    Secure Store Service

Security Token Service Application

User Profile App

    User Profile App

WSS_UsageApplication

    WSS_UsageApplication

If you do not have a Secure Store Service listed, you'll need to create one.

If you see a message at the top of the screen regarding a key, click the Generate New Key button from the top ribbon:

Enter a pass phrase and click OK:

Click New from the top ribbon:

Enter a Target Application ID, Display Name, and Contact E-mail:

You will need the Target Application ID to create the External Content Type. Click Next.

Change the Windows User Name field name to User ID the Windows Password field name to Password.

Change the associated Field Types from to User Name and Password. Click Next.

Enter Target Application Administrators and click OK:

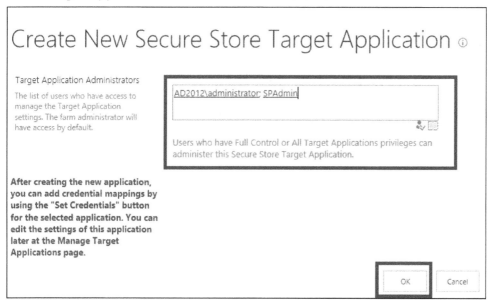

The Target Application entry is created:

Select the Target Application checkbox and click the Set Credentials button:

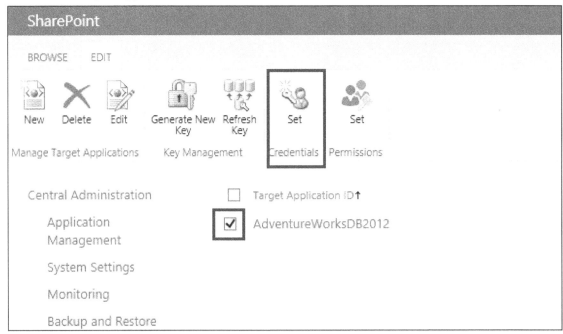

Enter the Credential Owner (this should be the service account that runs BCS), enter the SQL database User ID and Password. Click OK:

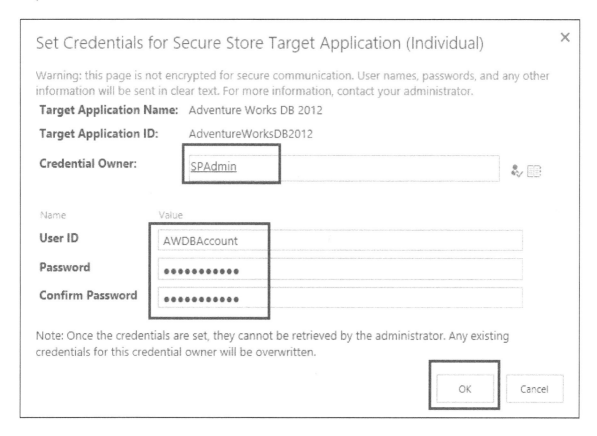

Step 3: Create an External Content Type

The methods here describe the steps for a no-code solution in creating an External Content Type that uses your data source as the provider of information via SharePoint Designer 2013.

Launch SharePoint Designer 2013 and open your Search Center site:

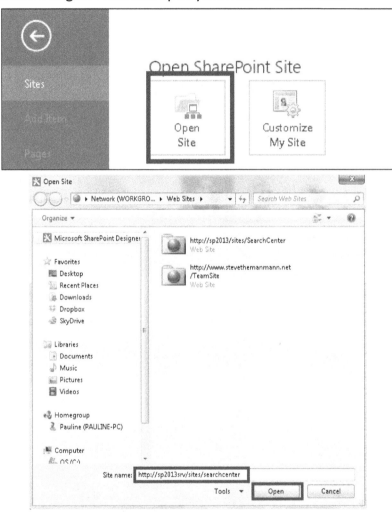

Click the External Content Types from the Site Objects and then click the External Content Type button from the top-ribbon:

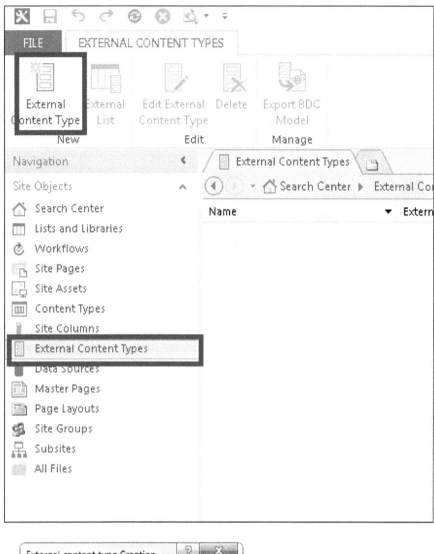

Enter a Name and Display Name and then click on the External System link:

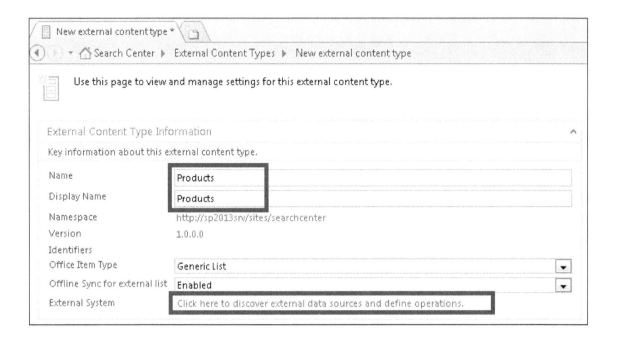

Click on the Add Connection button:

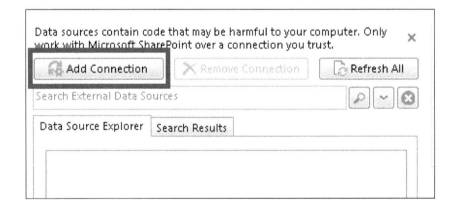

Select the type of connection. For this example, SQL Server is being used:

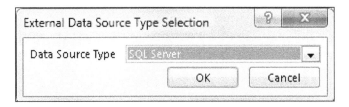

Click OK.

Enter the Database Server, the Database Name, and select Connect with Impersonated Custom Identity. Enter the Secure Store Application ID that was created in the previous section:

SQL Server Connection

Connection Properties

Database Server: SQLSRV2012

Database Name: AdventureWorks2012

Name (optional): Adventure Works 2012

○ Connect with User's Identity

○ Connect with Impersonated Windows Identity

◉ Connect with Impersonated Custom Identity

Secure Store Application ID: AdventureWorksDB2012

OK   Cancel

Click OK.

If prompted, enter SQL Server credentials to access the database.

Expand the database in the Data Source Explorer tab and then expand the Routines folder. Locate the Read List procedure, right click and select New Read List Operation:

Enter an Operation Name and Display Name.

The Operation Name becomes a prefix (ReadList.propertyname) in the crawled properties so it is a good idea to include an entity description in the name, otherwise it would be hard to distinguish crawled properties from their external content types.

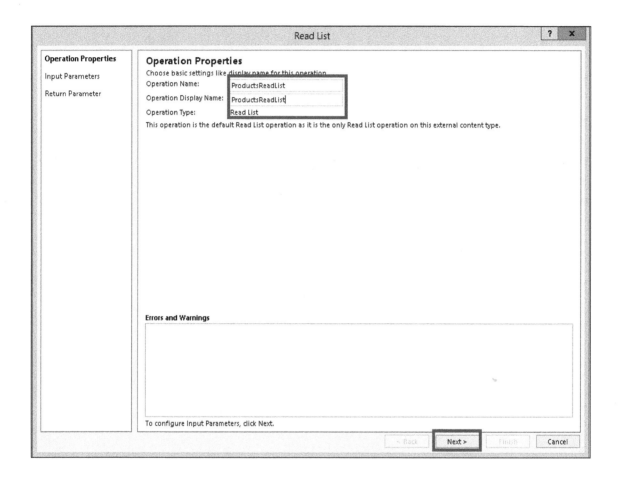

Click Next.

The example does not limit the Read List items and thus there are no Input Parameters. Click Next:

On the Return Parameter Configuration screen, make sure the row identifier (primary key) is selected and check the Map to Identifier checkbox. The Identifier, Field, and DisplayName become populated with the row identifier. Click Finish.

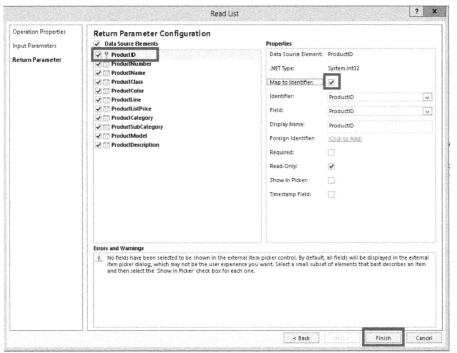

Next, locate the Read Item procedure, right click and select New Read Item Operation:

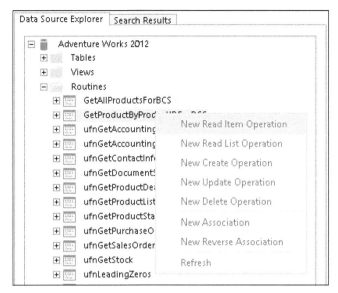

Enter appropriate operation names. Click Next:

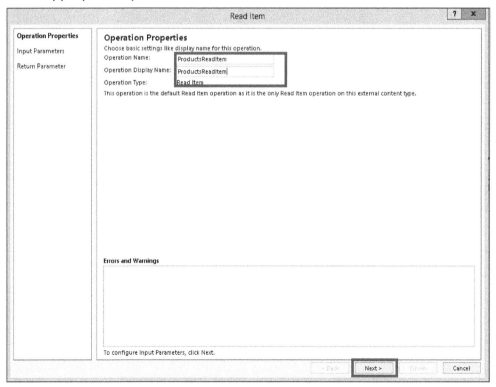

On the Input Parameters Configuration screen, make sure the input parameter is selected and the Map to Identifier is checked. Click Next:

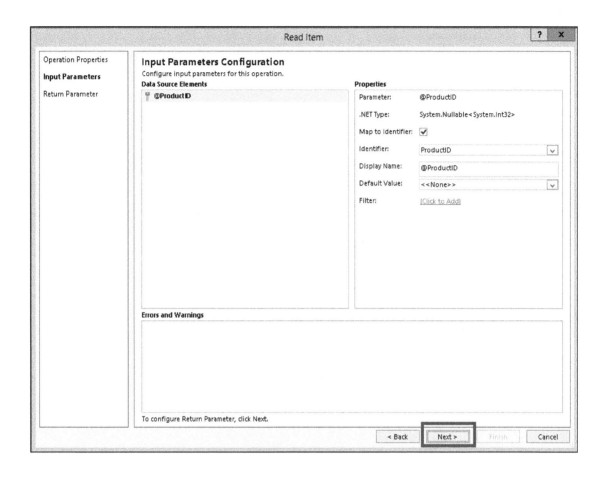

On the Return Parameter Configuration screen, make sure the row identifier (primary key) is selected and check the Map to Identifier checkbox. The Identifier, Field, and DisplayName become populated with the row identifier. Click Finish.

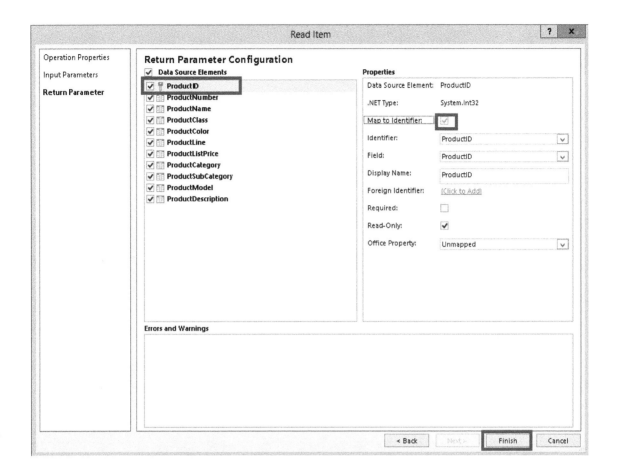

The new operations appear in the External Content Type Operations section:

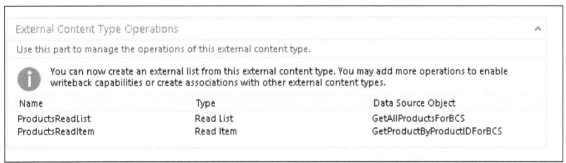

Save the External Content Type:

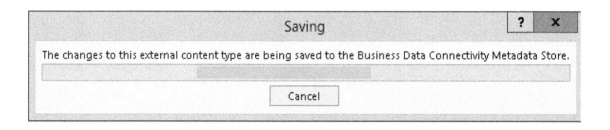

Keep SharePoint Designer 2013 open to the External Content Type. Navigate to your Business Data Connectivity Service Application and verify the new external content type exists:

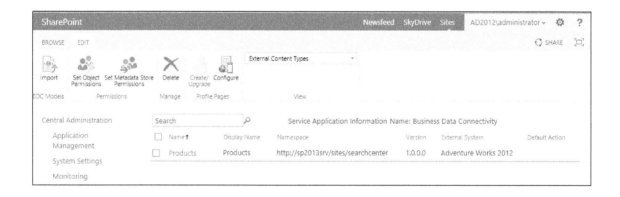

In your Business Data Connectivity Service Application, click the Configure button.

Enter a location to host the External Content Type profile pages:

It is recommended to use a dedicate SharePoint site. I personally like things being all together in my Search Center Site Collection so I use that.

Scroll down and click OK.

While you are here you could set the permissions in the BCS for the External Content type as explained in the next section (or just come back to it).

Navigate back to SharePoint Designer 2013 and with the External Content Type opened, click on the Create Profile Page button from the top-ribbon:

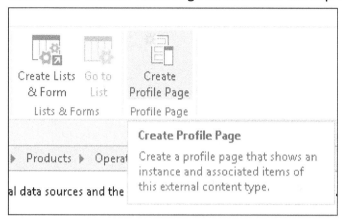

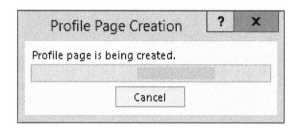

The Profile Page is created. This page becomes used for the search results URL if a custom URL (page) is not used as part of the data source.

Step 4: Set Permissions on the BCS Entity

Navigate to your Business Data Connectivity Service Application and select the External Content Type by checking the checkbox:

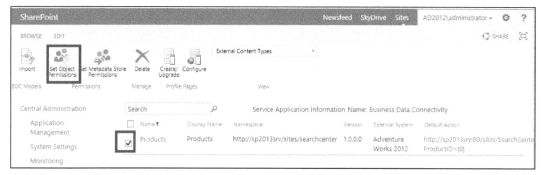

Click on the Set Object Permissions button from the top-ribbon.

Enter accounts into the account box (if your external content type is for general use include Everyone):

Click Add. Select each added account and check off the appropriate permissions. For Everyone, only check off Execute and Selectable In Clients.

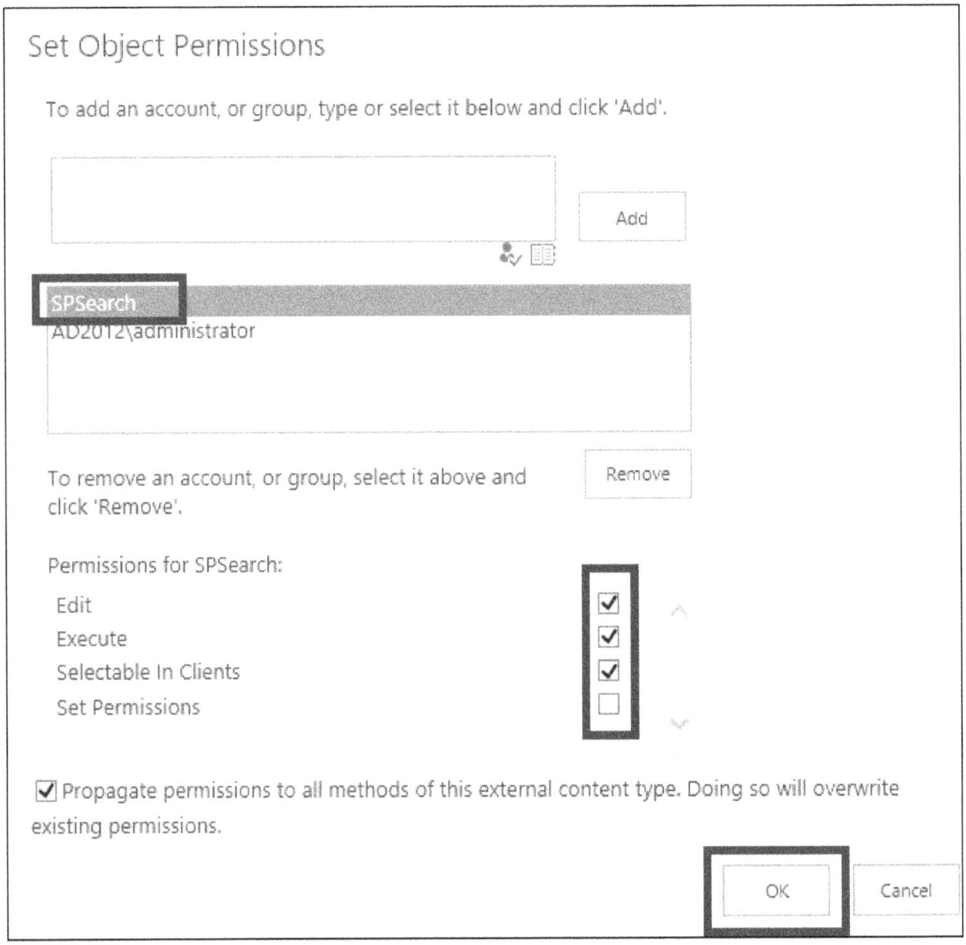

Set Object Permissions

To add an account, or group, type or select it below and click 'Add'.

	Add

SPSearch
AD2012\administrator

To remove an account, or group, select it above and click 'Remove'. Remove

Permissions for SPSearch:

Edit ☑
Execute ☑
Selectable In Clients ☑
Set Permissions ☐

☑ Propagate permissions to all methods of this external content type. Doing so will overwrite existing permissions.

OK   Cancel

Click OK.

Step 5: Create a Content Source for the External Content Type

Navigate to Central Administration and click on Manage service applications:

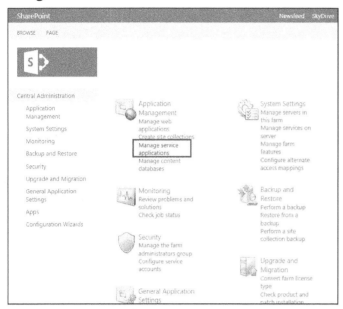

Click on the Search Service Application:

Click on Content Sources under Crawling (in the left hand column):

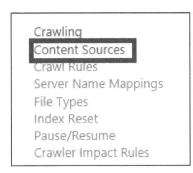

Crawling
Content Sources
Crawl Rules
Server Name Mappings
File Types
Index Reset
Pause/Resume
Crawler Impact Rules

On the Manage Content Source page click the New Content Source link:

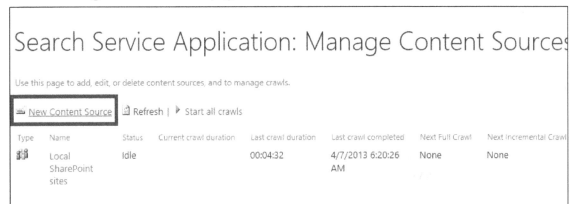

Search Service Application: Manage Content Sources

Use this page to add, edit, or delete content sources, and to manage crawls.

New Content Source | Refresh | ▶ Start all crawls

Type	Name	Status	Current crawl duration	Last crawl duration	Last crawl completed	Next Full Crawl	Next Incremental Crawl
	Local SharePoint sites	Idle		00:04:32	4/7/2013 6:20:26 AM	None	None

Enter a name for the Content Source and select Line of Business Data. Select the Crawl selected external data source and check off the data source:

Scroll down and click OK.

The content source is created and listed on the Manage Content Sources page:

Hover over the new content source and click the drop-down menu. Select Start Full Crawl:

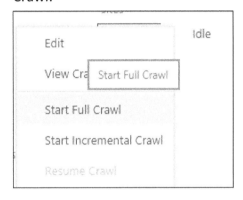

Step 6: Create Managed Properties Based on Crawled Properties

After the crawl has completed, you now need to create managed properties and map them to the crawled properties from the new content source. This may be accomplished from the Search Service Application UI or from PowerShell. Either way, you need to know what crawled properties have been created.

From the Search Service Application, click on Search Schema on the left hand side of the screen under Queries and Results:

On the Managed Properties page, click on Crawled Properties at the top:

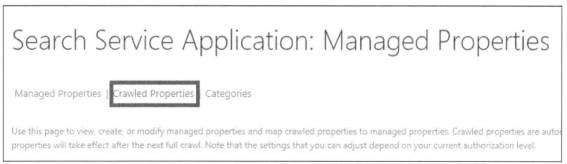

Select Business Data from the Category drop-down and click the filter button:

Filters

Crawled properties [   ]

Category [Business Data   ⌄]

☐ Show unaltered property names

[→]

The crawled properties from the external data source are displayed:

Total Count = 14

Property Name

docaclmeta

EntityName

EntityNamespace

ProductsReadListElement.ProductCategory

ProductsReadListElement.ProductClass

ProductsReadListElement.ProductColor

ProductsReadListElement.ProductDescription

ProductsReadListElement.ProductID

ProductsReadListElement.ProductLine

ProductsReadListElement.ProductListPrice

ProductsReadListElement.ProductModel

ProductsReadListElement.ProductName

ProductsReadListElement.ProductNumber

ProductsReadListElement.ProductSubCategory

You may also use PowerShell to list out the crawled properties. I use the following commands:

Add-PSSnapin Microsoft.SharePoint.PowerShell -ErrorAction SilentlyContinue

$ssa = Get-SPEnterpriseSearchServiceApplication

Get-SPEnterpriseSearchMetadataCrawledProperty -SearchApplication $ssa -Category 'Business Data' | ft Name

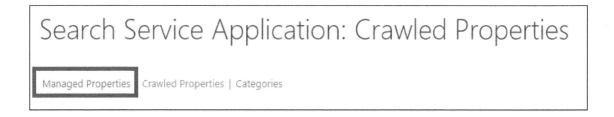

Now that you know what the crawled properties are, you can map them to managed properties. If the managed properties were already created, you could simply click on each crawled property on the Crawled Property page and map them. In this case, there are no managed properties yet.

Therefore click on the Managed Properties link at the top of the Crawled Properties page:

Search Service Application: Crawled Properties

Managed Properties | Crawled Properties | Categories

On the Managed Properties page, click on New Managed Property:

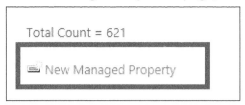

Enter a name for the property. I usually prefix them with the entity type so they are all displayed together and I know which content source they are from. Select the Type and check the Searchable checkbox:

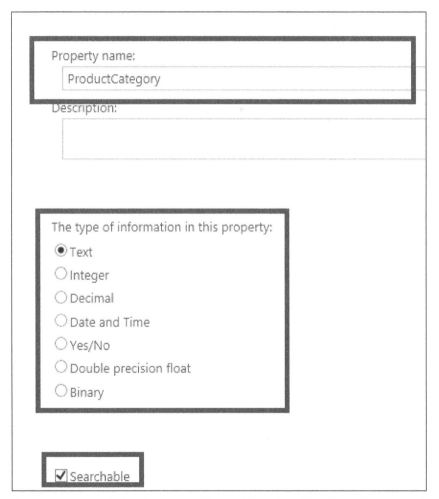

Scroll down and check Queryable and Retrievable. For this example, the Product Category will be refinable and sortable so I selected "Yes -active" for both of those entries:

Queryable:
Enables querying against the specific managed property. The managed property field name must be included in the query, either specified in the query itself or included in the query programmatically. If the managed property is "author", the query must contain "author:Smith".

☑ Queryable

Retrievable:
Enables the content of this managed property to be returned in search results. Enable this setting for managed properties that are relevant to present in search results.

☑ Retrievable

Allow multiple values:
Allow multiple values of the same type in this managed property. For example, if this is the "author" managed property, and a document has multiple authors, each author name will be stored as a separate value in this managed property.

☐ Allow multiple values

Refinable:
Yes - active: Enables using the property as a refiner for search results in the front end. You must manually configure the refiner in the web part.
Yes - latent: Enables switching refinable to active later, without having to do a full re-crawl when you switch.
Both options require a full crawl to take effect.

Refinable: Yes - active ▼

Sortable:
Yes - active: Enables sorting the result set based on the property before the result set is returned. Use for example for large result sets that cannot be sorted and retrieved at the same

Sortable: Yes - active ▼

For external content I usually select Include content from the first crawled property setting. These should be one-to-one mappings so it really doesn't make a difference. Click on the Add Mapping button:

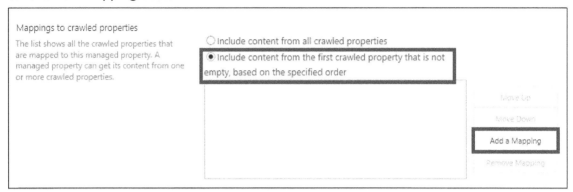

In the Crawled property dialog, select Business Data from the filter drop-down. Select the appropriate crawled property and click OK.

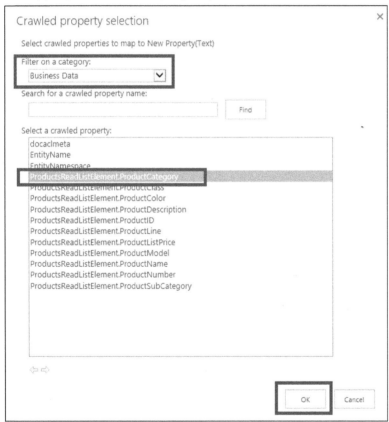

Back on the Add Managed Property page, click OK:

These managed properties are configured to be searchable, queryable, retrievable, sortable and refinable.	☐ Word Part Extraction - Custom5
	☐ Word Exact Extraction - Custom
	☐ Word Part Exact Extraction - Custom

OK   Cancel

You'll need to repeat this process for each crawled property.

Performing the mapping through the UI can become tedious. That's why I create a script to map all of my properties:

```
Add-PSSnapin Microsoft.SharePoint.PowerShell -ErrorAction SilentlyContinue
$ssa = Get-SPEnterpriseSearchServiceApplication

$crawledProperty = Get-SPEnterpriseSearchMetadataCrawledProperty -SearchApplication $ssa -Name ProductsReadListElement.ProductCategory
$managedProperty = New-SPEnterpriseSearchMetadataManagedProperty -SearchApplication $ssa -Name ProductCategory -FullTextQueriable:$true -Queryable:$true -Retrievable:$true -Type 1
New-SPEnterpriseSearchMetadataMapping -SearchApplication $ssa -ManagedProperty $managedProperty -CrawledProperty $crawledProperty
```

Just repeat the last three lines for each property mapping.

There are no parameters for sortable or refinable so I just go into the UI and change those settings manually for the properties I want to sort on or refine. You could create the crawled property if you knew what it was going to be named but in my script I get the crawled property since it was already created.

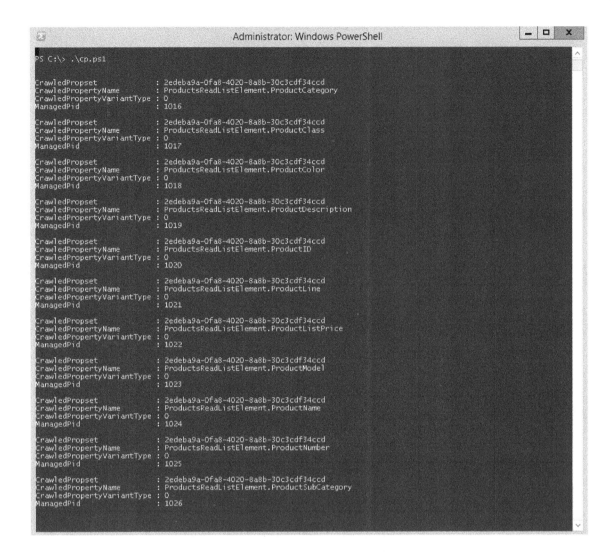

```
PS C:\> .\cp.ps1

CrawledPropset            : 2edeba9a-0fa8-4020-8a8b-30c3cdf34ccd
CrawledPropertyName       : ProductsReadListElement.ProductCategory
CrawledPropertyVariantType : 0
ManagedPid                : 1016

CrawledPropset            : 2edeba9a-0fa8-4020-8a8b-30c3cdf34ccd
CrawledPropertyName       : ProductsReadListElement.ProductClass
CrawledPropertyVariantType : 0
ManagedPid                : 1017

CrawledPropset            : 2edeba9a-0fa8-4020-8a8b-30c3cdf34ccd
CrawledPropertyName       : ProductsReadListElement.ProductColor
CrawledPropertyVariantType : 0
ManagedPid                : 1018

CrawledPropset            : 2edeba9a-0fa8-4020-8a8b-30c3cdf34ccd
CrawledPropertyName       : ProductsReadListElement.ProductDescription
CrawledPropertyVariantType : 0
ManagedPid                : 1019

CrawledPropset            : 2edeba9a-0fa8-4020-8a8b-30c3cdf34ccd
CrawledPropertyName       : ProductsReadListElement.ProductID
CrawledPropertyVariantType : 0
ManagedPid                : 1020

CrawledPropset            : 2edeba9a-0fa8-4020-8a8b-30c3cdf34ccd
CrawledPropertyName       : ProductsReadListElement.ProductLine
CrawledPropertyVariantType : 0
ManagedPid                : 1021

CrawledPropset            : 2edeba9a-0fa8-4020-8a8b-30c3cdf34ccd
CrawledPropertyName       : ProductsReadListElement.ProductListPrice
CrawledPropertyVariantType : 0
ManagedPid                : 1022

CrawledPropset            : 2edeba9a-0fa8-4020-8a8b-30c3cdf34ccd
CrawledPropertyName       : ProductsReadListElement.ProductModel
CrawledPropertyVariantType : 0
ManagedPid                : 1023

CrawledPropset            : 2edeba9a-0fa8-4020-8a8b-30c3cdf34ccd
CrawledPropertyName       : ProductsReadListElement.ProductName
CrawledPropertyVariantType : 0
ManagedPid                : 1024

CrawledPropset            : 2edeba9a-0fa8-4020-8a8b-30c3cdf34ccd
CrawledPropertyName       : ProductsReadListElement.ProductNumber
CrawledPropertyVariantType : 0
ManagedPid                : 1025

CrawledPropset            : 2edeba9a-0fa8-4020-8a8b-30c3cdf34ccd
CrawledPropertyName       : ProductsReadListElement.ProductSubCategory
CrawledPropertyVariantType : 0
ManagedPid                : 1026
```

In order for the Managed Properties to take effect, you now need to run a full crawl on the content source again.

Step 7: Create a Result Source for the New Content Source

Navigate to your Search Center and select Site Settings from the Settings menu:

Under the Site Collection Administration section, click on Search Result Sources:

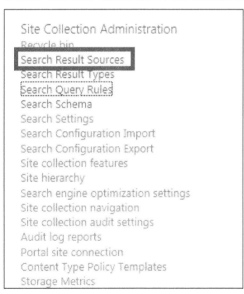

On the Manage Result Sources page, click on the New Result Source link:

On the Add Result Source page, enter a name for the Result Source. For this example, I am using Products:

Scroll down and click on the Launch Query Builder button:

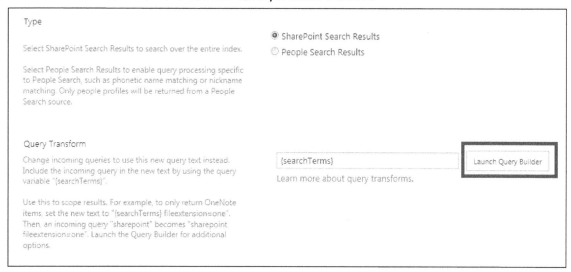

In the Property Filter section, first select "--Show all managed properties--":

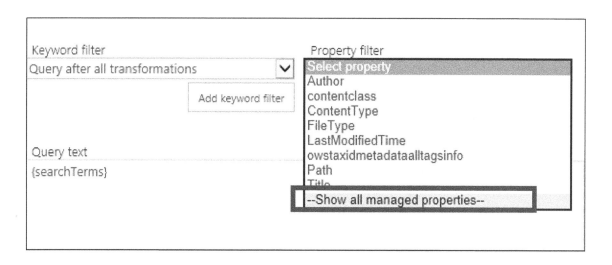

Next select ContentSource from the drop-down. Select Equals and Manual value:

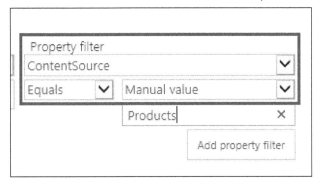

Enter the name of the content source (e.g. Products) in the text box and click Add property filter:

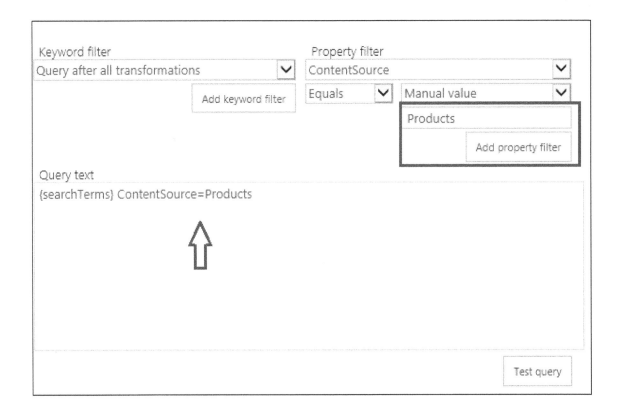

The property filter is added to the Query text.

Click OK on the Build Your Query dialog.

The property filter is added to the Query Transform text box.

Click Save:

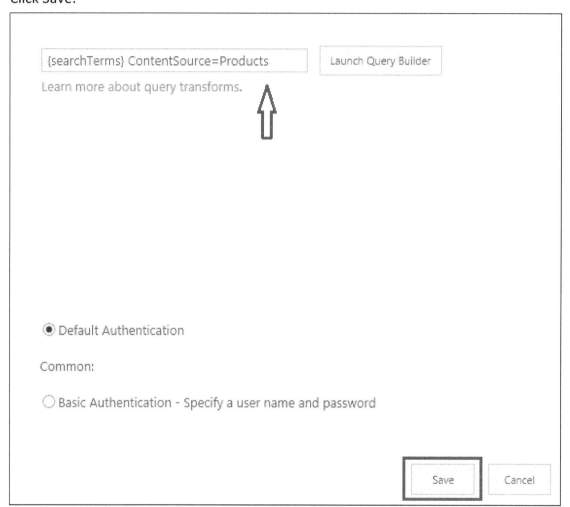

The new result source is created and appears under the Defined for this site section:

Site Collection Administration

Use result sources to scope search results and federate queries to exter

Result Sources replace Search Scopes, which are now deprecated. You

New Result Source

Name

Defined for this site collection (1)

Products

Provided by SharePoint (16)

Step 8: Create a Result Type for the Result Source

Navigate to your Search Center and select Site Settings from the Settings menu.

Under the Site Collection Administration section, click on the Search Result Types link:

Site Collection Administration
Recycle bin
Search Result Sources
Search Result Types
Search Query Rules
Search Schema
Search Settings
Search Configuration Import
Search Configuration Export
Site collection features
Site hierarchy
Search engine optimization settings
Site collection navigation

On the Result Types page click on the New Result Type link:

Enter a name for the Result Type. Select the Result Source created in the previous section from the source drop-down. Skip the types of content rule. Select Default Item for now under "What should these results look like?". You will create a custom item template in later sections.

Site Collection Administration › Add Result Type

apply to all sites in the site collection. To make one for just this site, use site result types.

Give it a name

Products

Which source should results match?

Products ⌄

What types of content should match? You can skip this rule to match all content

Select a value ⌄

Add value

What should these results look like?

Default Item ⌄

Note: This result type will automatically update with the latest properties in your display template each time you visit the Manage Result Types Page.

Display template URL

~sitecollection/_catalogs/masterpage/Display Templates/Search/Item_Default.js

☐ Optimize for frequent use

Save   Cancel

Click Save.

Step 9: Create a Search Results Page for the New Content Source

Navigate to your Search Center and select Site Contents from the Settings menu:

Locate and double-click the Pages library:

From the Files tab in the top ribbon, select Page from the New Document drop-down menu:

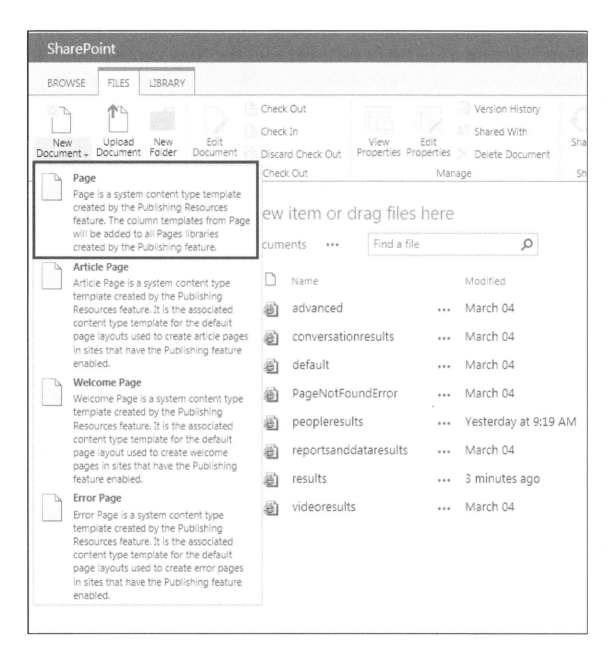

On the Create Page page, enter a title and URL Name. Click Create.

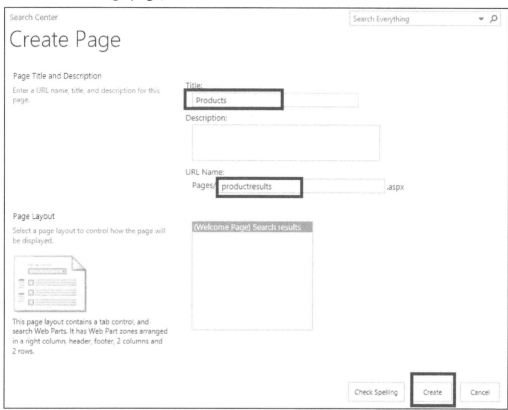

Select the ellipsis menu on the new page and click on OPEN:

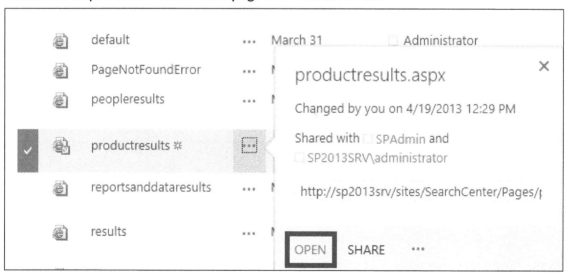

From the Settings menu select Edit page:

Locate the Search Results web part and select Edit Web Part from the drop-down menu:

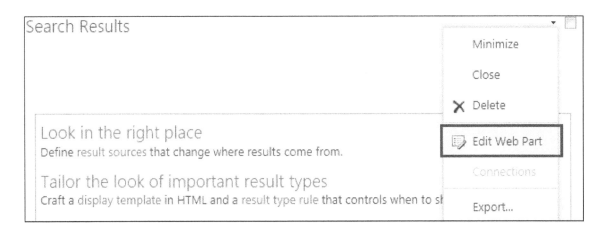

In the Properties tool pane that appeared on the right, click the Change query button:

The Build Your Query dialog appears.

In the Select a query section, select the custom Result Source created in the previous section of this chapter:

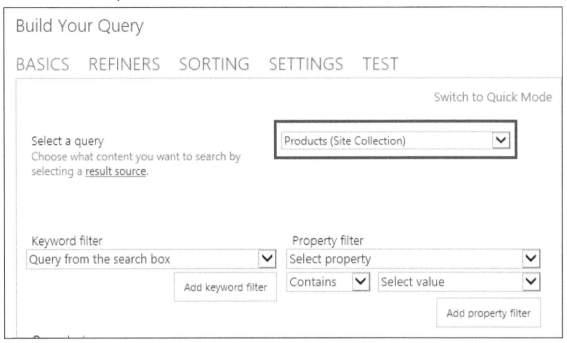

Click OK on the Build Your Query dialog.

Click OK in the web part properties tool pane:

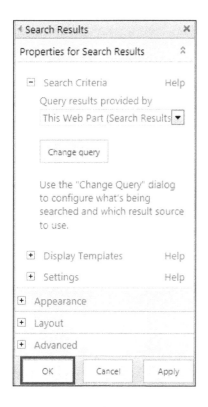

Check in the page:

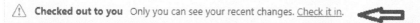

Publish the page:

-

Step 10: Add a Custom Results Page to the Search Center Navigation

Navigate to your Search Center and select Site Settings from the Settings menu:

Under the Search section click the Search Settings link:

At the bottom the Search Settings page, click on Add Link...:

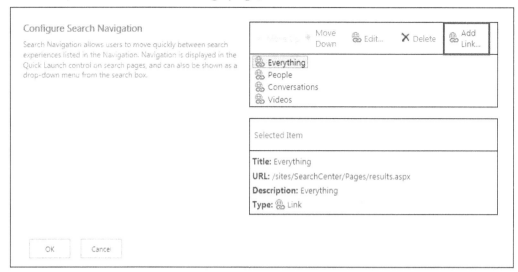

Enter a title and the URL to the custom page that was created in the previous section. Click OK.

Navigation Link   ✕

Edit the title, URL, and description of the navigation item.

Title: Products

URL: Center/Pages/productresults.aspx ✕   Browse...

☐ Open link in new window

Description:

Audience:

OK   Cancel

Back on the Search Settings page click OK:

Configure Search Navigation

Search Navigation allows users to move quickly between search experiences listed in the Navigation. Navigation is displayed in the Quick Launch control on search pages, and can also be shown as a drop-down menu from the search box.

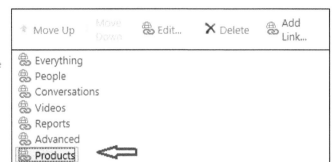

⬆ Move Up   Move Down   🌐 Edit...   ✕ Delete   🌐 Add Link...

🌐 Everything
🌐 People
🌐 Conversations
🌐 Videos
🌐 Reports
🌐 Advanced
🌐 Products ⬅

Selected Item

Title: Products
URL: /sites/SearchCenter/Pages/productresults.aspx
Description:
Type: 🌐 Link

OK   Cancel

Step 11: Test the Results

Navigate to your Search Center. The new navigation item appears at the top. Click on the new link and perform a search:

The results aren't too pretty. The next section explains how to create custom item templates and hover panels for the external content source.

Step 12: Create an Item Display Template

Fire up SharePoint Designer 2013 and Open the Search Center Site:

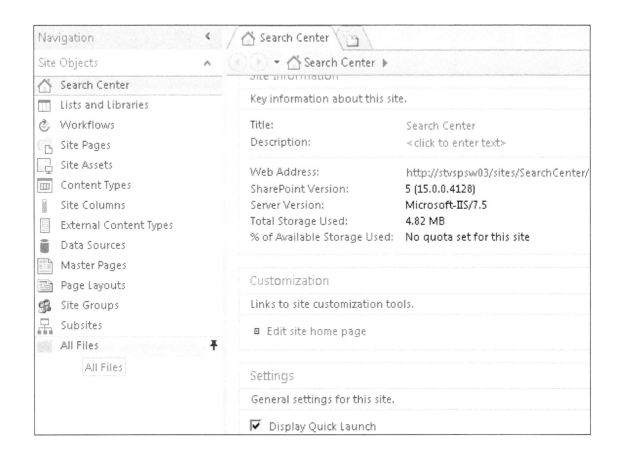

Click on All Files from the left-hand navigation:

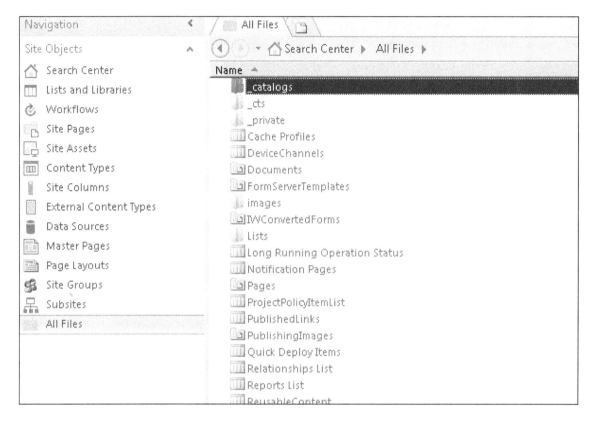

A list of all files is displayed in the main window.

If you attempt to get the files from the Master Pages object, you will not see any items once you get to the Display Templates folders.

Double-click on the _catalogs folder in the main window

This action displays the _catalogs structure under the left-hand navigation.

Expand the _catalogs folder, then the masterpage folder, and then the Display Templates folder.

Click on the Search folder under Display Templates:

The list of Search display templates is shown in the main window area.

Locate Item_Default.html and Item_Default.js. Select both files, right-click, and select copy:

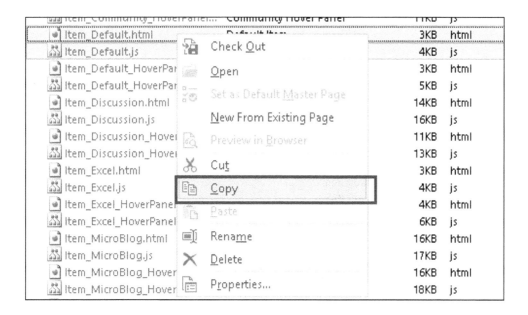

Right click again and select Paste:

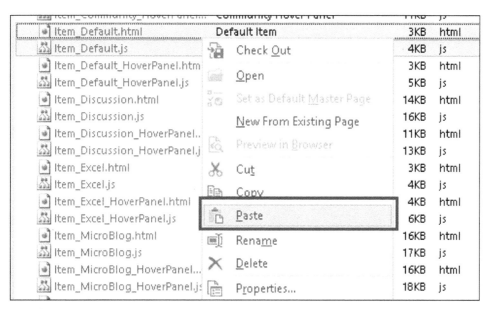

The files are copied in place.

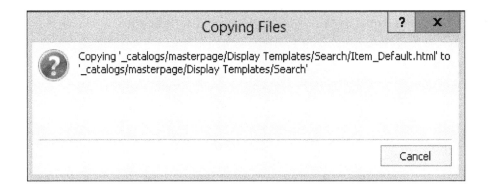

Rename the html copy:

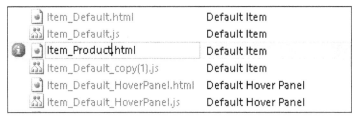

SharePoint automatically renames the .js file:

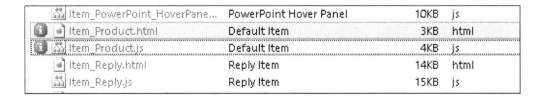

Right-click the html file and select Edit File in Advanced Mode:

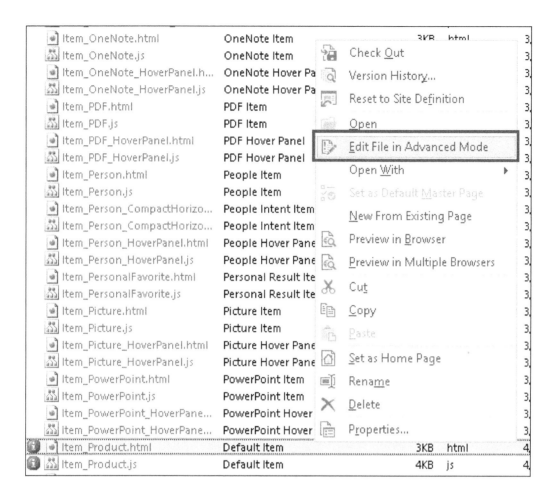

Rename the title:

```
1 <html xmlns:mso="urn:schemas-microsoft-com:office:office" xmlns:
2 <head>
3 <title>Product Item</title>          <=
4
5 <!--[if gte mso 9]><xml>
6 <mso:CustomDocumentProperties>
7 <mso:TemplateHidden msdt:dt="string">0</mso:TemplateHidden>
```

Add the external content type managed properties to the ManagedProperties tag:

```
<mso:ManagedPropertyMapping msdt:dt="string">&#39;ProductSubCategory&#39;:&#39;ProductSubCategory&#39;,&#39;ProductNumber&#39;:&#39;ProductNumber&#39;,&#39;
```

'ProductSubCategory':'ProductSubCategory','ProductNumber':'Product Number',

(see code examples on www.SteveTheManMann.com)

In the javascript code block, rename the hover panel:

```
if(!$isNull(ctx.CurrentItem) && !$isNull(ctx.ClientControl)){
    var id = ctx.ClientControl.get_nextUniqueId();
    var itemId = id + Srch.U.Ids.item;
    var hoverId = id + Srch.U.Ids.hover;
    var hoverUrl = "~sitecollection/_catalogs/masterpage/Display Templates/Search/Item_Product_HoverPanel.js";
    $setResultItem(itemId, ctx.CurrentItem);
    if(ctx.CurrentItem.IsContainer){
        ctx.CurrentItem.csr_Icon = Srch.U.getFolderIconUrl();
    }
    ctx.currentItem_ShowHoverPanelCallback = Srch.U.getShowHoverPanelCallback(itemId, hoverId, hoverUrl);
    ctx.currentItem_HideHoverPanelCallback = Srch.U.getHideHoverPanelCallback();
```

You will create the hover panel file in the next section.

Rename the data-displaytemplate:

```
<div id="_#= $htmlEncode(itemId) =#_" name="Item" data-displaytemplate="ProductItem" class=
    _#=ctx.RenderBody(ctx)=#_
    <div id="_#= $htmlEncode(hoverId) =#_" class="ms-srch-hover-outerContainer"></div>
</div>
```

In the javascript code block, I create variables that determine if there is data in the managed property fields:

```
<!--#_
    if(!$isNull(ctx.CurrentItem) && !$isNull(ctx.ClientControl)){
        var id = ctx.ClientControl.get_nextUniqueId();
        var itemId = id + Srch.U.Ids.item;
        var hoverId = id + Srch.U.Ids.hover;
        var hoverUrl = "~sitecollection/_catalogs/masterpage/Display Templates/Search/Item_Product_HoverPanel.js";
        $setResultItem(itemId, ctx.CurrentItem);
        if(ctx.CurrentItem.IsContainer){
            ctx.CurrentItem.csr_Icon = Srch.U.getFolderIconUrl();
        }

        var has_name = !$isEmptyString(ctx.CurrentItem.ProductName);
        var has_model = !$isEmptyString(ctx.CurrentItem.ProductModel);
        var has_number = !$isEmptyString(ctx.CurrentItem.ProductNumber);
        var has_category = !$isEmptyString(ctx.CurrentItem.ProductCategory);

        ctx.currentItem_ShowHoverPanelCallback = Srch.U.getShowHoverPanelCallback(itemId, hoverId, hoverUrl);
        ctx.currentItem_HideHoverPanelCallback = Srch.U.getHideHoverPanelCallback();
_#-->
```

var has_name = !$isEmptyString(ctx.CurrentItem.ProductName);

var has_model = !$isEmptyString(ctx.CurrentItem.ProductModel);

var has_number = !$isEmptyString(ctx.CurrentItem.ProductNumber);

var has_category = !$isEmptyString(ctx.CurrentItem.ProductCategory);

Remove the ctx.RenderBody line:

```
        <div id="_#= $htmlEncode(itemId) =#_" name="I
            _#=ctx.RenderBody(ctx)=#_
            <div id="_#= $htmlEncode(hoverId) =#_" cl
        </div>
<!--#_
    }
_#-->
```

For each managed property, create a code block similar to the following:

```
<!--#
        if(has_number == true) {
#-->
            <div id="ProductNumberField">
                <div id="ProductNumberValue" class="ms-srch-ellipsis" title="_#= ctx.CurrentItem.ProductNumber =#_">Product Number:  _#= ctx.CurrentItem.ProductNumber =#_ </div>
            </div>
<!--#
        }
#-->
```

<!--#

            if(has_number == true) {

 #-->

                          <div id="ProductNumberValue" class="ms-srch-ellipsis" title="_#=
ctx.CurrentItem.ProductNumber =#_">Product Number: _#= ctx.CurrentItem.ProductNumber =#_

<!--#

            }

 #-->

Code examples are available on www.SteveTheManMann.com.

```
<div id="_#= $htmlEncode(itemId) =#_" name="Item" data-displaytemplate="ProductItem" class="ms-srch-item" onmouseover="_#= ctx.currentItem_ShowHoverPanelCallback =#_" onmouseout="_#=
    if(has_number == true) {
        <div id="ProductNumberField">
            <div id="ProductNumberValue" class="ms-srch-ellipsis" title="_#= ctx.CurrentItem.ProductNumber =#_">Product Number:  _#= ctx.CurrentItem.ProductNumber =#_ </div>
        </div>
    }

    if(has_name == true) {
        <div id="ProductNameField">
            <div id="ProductNameValue" class="ms-srch-ellipsis" title="_#= ctx.CurrentItem.ProductName =#_">Product Name:  _#= ctx.CurrentItem.ProductName =#_ </div>
        </div>
    }

    if(has_model == true) {
        <div id="ProductModelField">
            <div id="ProductModelValue" class="ms-srch-ellipsis" title="_#= ctx.CurrentItem.ProductModel =#_">Product Model:  _#= ctx.CurrentItem.ProductModel =#_ </div>
        </div>
    }
```

Save the html file.

Step 13: Create an Item Hover Panel

Back in the listing of display templates, locate and select the Item_Default_HoverPanel files. Right-click and select Copy:

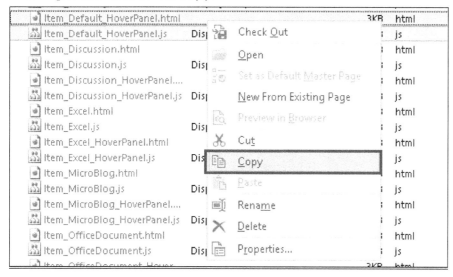

Right-click again and select Paste:

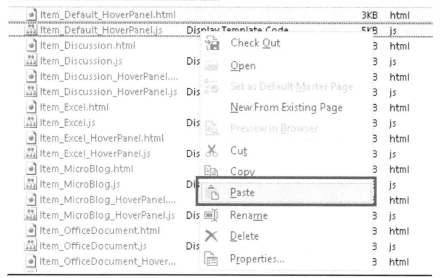

Rename the html file:

SharePoint automatically renames the .js file:

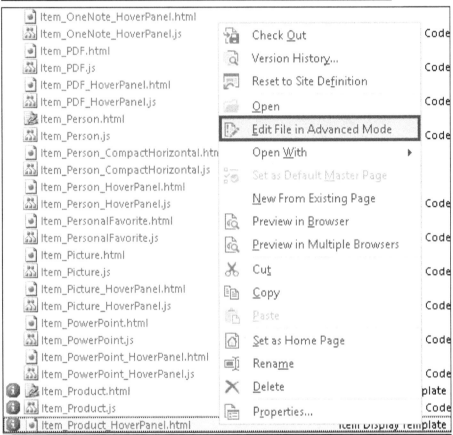

Item_Product.html		Item Display Template
Item_Product.js		Display Template Code
Item_Product_HoverPanel.html		Item Display Template
Item_Product_HoverPanel.js		Display Template Code

Right click the html file and select Edit File in Advanced Mode:

Item_OneNote_HoverPanel.html		
Item_OneNote_HoverPanel.js	Check Out	Code
Item_PDF.html	Version History...	
Item_PDF.js	Reset to Site Definition	Code
Item_PDF_HoverPanel.html	Open	Code
Item_PDF_HoverPanel.js		
Item_Person.html	**Edit File in Advanced Mode**	Code
Item_Person.js	Open With ▶	
Item_Person_CompactHorizontal.htm	Set as Default Master Page	
Item_Person_CompactHorizontal.js	New From Existing Page	
Item_Person_HoverPanel.html		Code
Item_Person_HoverPanel.js	Preview in Browser	
Item_PersonalFavorite.html	Preview in Multiple Browsers	Code
Item_PersonalFavorite.js		
Item_Picture.html	Cut	Code
Item_Picture.js	Copy	
Item_Picture_HoverPanel.html	Paste	Code
Item_Picture_HoverPanel.js		
Item_PowerPoint.html	Set as Home Page	Code
Item_PowerPoint.js	Rename	
Item_PowerPoint_HoverPanel.html	Delete	Code
Item_PowerPoint_HoverPanel.js		
Item_Product.html	Properties...	plate
Item_Product.js		Code
Item_Product_HoverPanel.html		Item Display Template

Rename the title:

```
1 <html xmlns:mso="urn:schemas-microsoft-com:office:office"
2 <head>
3 <title>Product Hover Panel</title>
4
5 <!--[if gte mso 9]><xml>
6 <mso:CustomDocumentProperties>
```

Copy and paste the ManagedPropertyMapping from the item display template created in the previous section:

```
<!--[if gte mso 9]><xml>
<mso:CustomDocumentProperties>
<mso:TemplateHidden msdt:dt="string">0</mso:TemplateHidden>
<mso:MasterPageDescription msdt:dt="string">Displays the default hover panel template.</mso:MasterPageDescription>
<mso:ContentTypeId msdt:dt="string">0x0101002039C03B61C64EC4A04F5361F385106603</mso:ContentTypeId>
<mso:TargetControlType msdt:dt="string">;#SearchHoverPanel;#</mso:TargetControlType>
<mso:HtmlDesignAssociated msdt:dt="string">1</mso:HtmlDesignAssociated>
<mso:ManagedPropertyMapping msdt:dt="string">'ProductSubCategory':'ProductSubCategory','ProductNumber':'
'Title':'Title','Path':'Path','Description':'Description','EditorOWSUSER':'
<mso:HtmlDesignConversionSucceeded msdt:dt="string">True</mso:HtmlDesignConversionSucceeded>
<mso:HtmlDesignStatusAndPreview msdt:dt="string">http://sp2013srv/sites/SearchCenter/_catalogs/masterpage/Display%20Templates/Search/
</mso:CustomDocumentProperties>
```

Rename the Default entries:

```
<body>
    <div id="Item Product HoverPanel">
<!--#_
        var i = 0;
        var id = ctx.CurrentItem.csr_id;
        ctx.CurrentItem.csr_ShowViewLibrary = !Srch.U.isWebPage(ctx.CurrentItem.FileExtension);
        if(ctx.CurrentItem.IsContainer)
        {
            ctx.CurrentItem.csr_FileType = Srch.Res.ct_Folder
        }

        ctx.currentItem_ShowChangedBySnippet = true;

_#-->
        <div class="ms-srch-hover-innerContainer ms-srch-hover-standardSize" id="_#= $htmlEncode(id + HP.ids.inner) =#_">
            <div class="ms-srch-hover-arrowBorder" id="_#= $htmlEncode(id + HP.ids.arrowBorder) =#_"></div>
            <div class="ms-srch-hover-arrow" id="_#= $htmlEncode(id + HP.ids.arrow) =#_"></div>
            <div class="ms-srch-hover-content" id="_#= $htmlEncode(id + HP.ids.content) =#_" data-displaytemplate="ProductHoverPanel">
                <div id="_#= $htmlEncode(id + HP.ids.header) =#_" class="ms-srch-hover-header">
                    _#= ctx.RenderHeader(ctx) =#_
```

Create variables for the managed properties you wish to display in the hover panel:

```
var has_name = !$isEmptyString(ctx.CurrentItem.ProductName);
var has_description = !$isEmptyString(ctx.CurrentItem.ProductDescription);
var has_color = !$isEmptyString(ctx.CurrentItem.ProductColor);
var has_listprice = !$isEmptyString(ctx.CurrentItem.ProductListPrice);
var has_category = !$isEmptyString(ctx.CurrentItem.ProductCategory);
var has_subcategory = !$isEmptyString(ctx.CurrentItem.ProductSubCategory);
```

Remove the Render Header <div>:

```
<div class="ms-srch-hover-content" id="_#= $htmlEncode(id + HP.ids.content) =#_" data-displaytemplate="ProductHoverPanel">
    <div id="_#= $htmlEncode(id + HP.ids.header) =#_" class="ms-srch-hover-header">
        _#= ctx.RenderHeader(ctx) =#_
    </div>
    <div id="_#= $htmlEncode(id + HP.ids.body) =#_" class="ms-srch-hover-body">
<!--#_
```

Remove the ctx.RenderBody line:

```
<div class="ms-srch-hover-innerContainer ms-srch-hover-star
    <div class="ms-srch-hover-arrowBorder" id="_#= $htmlEnc
    <div class="ms-srch-hover-arrow" id="_#= $htmlEncode(id
    <div class="ms-srch-hover-content" id="_#= $htmlEncode
        <div id="_#= $htmlEncode(id + HP.ids.header) =#_"
            _#= ctx.RenderHeader(ctx) =#_
        </div>
        <div id="_#= $htmlEncode(id + HP.ids.body) =#_" cl
            _#= ctx.RenderBody(ctx) =#_
        </div>
        <div id="_#= $htmlEncode(id + HP.ids.actions) =#_"
            _#= ctx.RenderFooter(ctx) =#_
        </div>
    </div>
</div>
```

Again, add code blocks for each managed property. Example files are located on
www.SteveTheManMann.com:

```
<div id="_#= $htmlEncode(id + HP.ids.body) =#_" class="ms-srch-hover-body">

    if(has_name == true) {

        <div id="ProductNameField">
            <div id="ProductNameValue" class="ms-srch-ellipsis" style="font-weight:bold"
        </div>

    }


    if(has_description == true) {

        <div id="ProductDescriptionField">
            <div id="ProductDescriptionValue" class="ms-srch-ellipsis" title="_#= ctx.Cur
        </div>

    }



    if(has_color == true) {

        <div id="ProductColorField">
            <div id="ProductColorValue" class="ms-srch-ellipsis" title="_#= ctx.CurrentI
        </div>

    }
```

Save the file.

Step 14: Update the Result Type to Use the New Display Template

Navigate to your Search Center and select Site Settings from the Settings menu.

Under the Site Collection Administration section, click on the Search Result Types link:

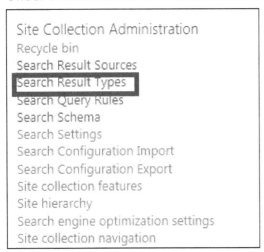

Locate the external content type Result Type and select Edit from the drop-down menu:

Change the What should these results look like? to the new display template created in the previous sections:

Site Collection Administration › Edit Result Type

Give it a name

Products

Which source should results match?

Products ▾

What types of content should match? You can skip this rule to match all content

Select a value ▾

Add value

What should these results look like?

Product Item ▾

Note: This result type will automatically update with the latest properties in your display template each time you visit the Manage Result Types Page.

Display template URL

~sitecollection/_catalogs/masterpage/Display Templates/Search/Item_Product.js

☐ Optimize for frequent use

Save   Cancel

Click Save.

Step 15: Test the Item Display Template and Hover Panel

Navigate to your Search Center and perform a search within the new results page:

The results are shown with the managed property values and the hover panel displays additional information.

Conclusion

This guide demonstrated an end-to-end solution involving the integration of external data from SQL Server into SharePoint 2013 leveraging Business Data Connectivity Services. I hope you found this guide helpful and easy to follow. If there are any questions, issues, or concerns, please send them to steve@stevethemanmann.com.

Volume 3

How To Enhance Video Search Results in SharePoint 2013

STEVEN MANN

How To Enhance Video Search Results in SharePoint 2013

Copyright © 2013 by Steven Mann

Trademarks

Screenshots of Microsoft Products and Services

Warning and Disclaimer

Introduction

This guide explains some easy and simple options that you may wish to incorporate into your search center to enhance the querying and display of video based search results in SharePoint 2013.

Reference links and source code are available on www.stevethemanmann.com:

Implementing a Videos Query Rule

In SharePoint 2013 Search there are several out-of-the-box query rules to display ranked result blocks of various result types (.e.g Word, Excel, PowerPoint, etc.). These are triggered based on specific action terms that appear either in the beginning or end of a search query (or both). However, Videos is not one of them.

Therefore, it would be nice if someone performed a search query using "video" or "videos" that a promoted result block of video results would appear at the top of the results. Easier done than said!

Navigate to your Site Settings from within your Search Center site collection and click on Search Query Rules under Site Collection Administration:

Select Local SharePoint Results (System) as the Result Source:

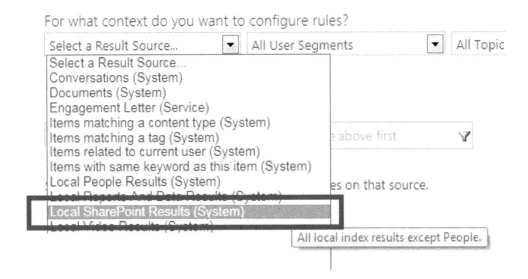

Click on the New Query Rule link:

Add the Rule Name, select Query Contains Action Term, enter "video;videos" in the Action term is one of these phrases:

Click on Add Result Block.

Modify the Block Title. Change Search this Source to Local Video Results (System) and increase the amount of Items as desired (I used 6). Expand the Settings section.

Select the "More" link since there is already a Video Results page and enter the value shown in the image below. Select Video Item as the Display Template:

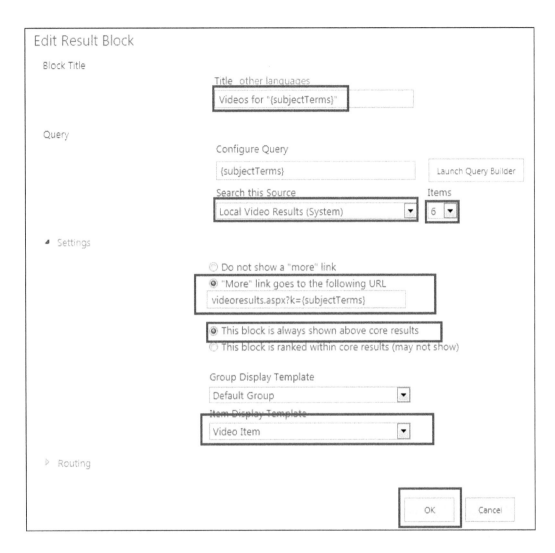

Click OK and then click Save on the New Query Rule page.

Navigate to your Search Center main page and perform a search using "videos" in the query:

Videos for "sharepoint"

SharePoint Youtube

/Video Library/SharePoint Youtube

SharePoint in Plain English

Mann, Steven Enterprise App Engineer, Application
Development ...

/Videos/SharePoint in Plain English

SharePoint Video

/sites/Videos/Videos/SharePoint Video

What is SharePoint

Mann, Steven Enterprise App Engineer, Application
Development ...

/sites/Videos/Videos/What is SharePoint

Top Benefits of SharePoint 2013

Mann, Steven Enterprise App Engineer, Application
Development ...

/sites/.../Videos/Top Benefits of SharePoint 2013

Tour SharePoint 2013 User Interfaces

Mann, Steven Enterprise App Engineer, Application
Development ...

/sites/.../Tour SharePoint 2013 User Interfaces

The video result block appears at the top and displays the video results. The results show hover panels when moused over.

Display Video Results Horizontally

There is another way to display these results using an out-of-the-box horizontal video display template. If you go back into your Search Query Rules, edit the Video query, and then edit the Result Block, you may change the Display Template setting to just the Video entry:

Now the results are displayed horizontally along the top:

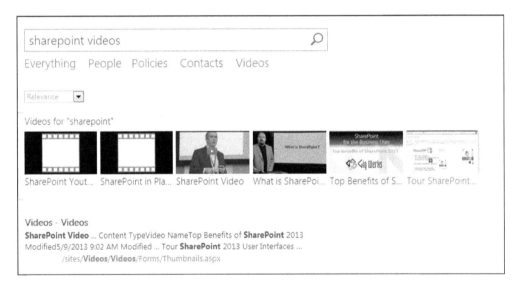

This presents well but there is no hover! You can easily modify the template (or make a new copy as the recommended approach) to display the hover. Those steps are in the next section.

Adding a Hover Panel to the Video Horizontal Display Template

The previous section demonstrated how to display Video results in a horizontal fashion using the out-of-the-box Video horizontal template. However, this display does not incorporate a hover panel and thus nothing pops up when mousing over the results. No problem. You may add a hover panel to the template in just a few easy steps.

First, navigate to the Search Center display templates via SharePoint Designer 2013, similar to the process explained in Appendix A. For simplicity, these steps discuss modifying the display template file in-place but the recommended approach would be to make a copy and use that.

Locate the Item_Video_CompactHorizontal.html file, right-click, and select Edit File in Advanced Mode:

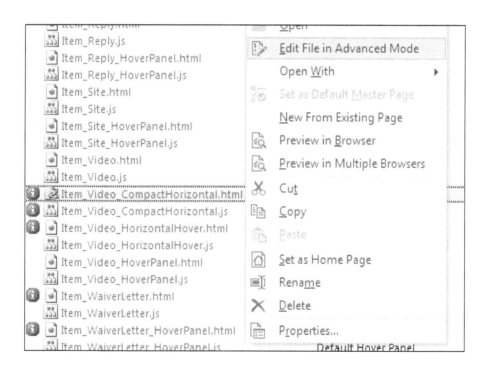

Paste this code at the top as shown in the image below:

```
var id = ctx.ClientControl.get_nextUniqueId();
var itemId = id + Srch.U.Ids.item;
var hoverId = id + Srch.U.Ids.hover;
var hoverUrl = "~sitecollection/_catalogs/masterpage/Display Templates/Search/Item_Video_HoverPanel.js";
$setResultItem(itemId, ctx.CurrentItem);
ctx.currentItem_ShowHoverPanelCallback = Srch.U.getShowHoverPanelCallback(itemId, hoverId, hoverUrl);
ctx.currentItem_HideHoverPanelCallback = Srch.U.getHideHoverPanelCallback();
```

```
</head>
<body>

    <div id="Item_Video_CompactHorizontal">
<!--#_

var id = ctx.ClientControl.get_nextUniqueId();
var itemId = id + Srch.U.Ids.item;
var hoverId = id + Srch.U.Ids.hover;
var hoverUrl = "~sitecollection/_catalogs/masterpage/Display Templates/Search/Item_Video_HoverPanel.js";
$setResultItem(itemId, ctx.CurrentItem);
ctx.currentItem_ShowHoverPanelCallback = Srch.U.getShowHoverPanelCallback(itemId, hoverId, hoverUrl);
ctx.currentItem_HideHoverPanelCallback = Srch.U.getHideHoverPanelCallback();

var encodedId = $htmlEncode(ctx.ClientControl.get_nextUniqueId());
var containerId = encodedId + "_videoIntentContainer";
var viewsId = encodedId + "_videoIntentViewsLifeTime";
var pathId = encodedId + "_videoIntentPath";
var line1Id = encodedId + "_videoIntentLine1";
```

Notice this is using the out-of-the-box Item_Video_HoverPanel .

Next, scroll down to the main <div> and change the id to use _#= $htmlEncode(itemId) =#_

```
mediaDuration.overrideValueRenderer(formatTimeFromSeconds);
_#-->
        <div class="ms-srch-video-intent ms-srch-video-intent-container" id="_#= $htmlEncode(itemId) =#_" data-displaytemplate="VideoIntentIt
            <div id="_#= $htmlEncode(hoverId) =#_" class="ms-srch-hover-outerContainer"></div>
            <div class="ms-srch-video-results-centered ms-srch-video-intent">
                <a clicktype="Result" href="_#= linkUrl =#_" title="_#= $htmlEncode(line1.value) =#_" id="_#= pathId =#_">
                    _#= imageMarkup =#_
                </a>
            </div>
            <div class="ms-srch-video-intent-data">
                <h3>
                    <a clicktype="Result" href="_#= linkUrl =#_" title="_#= $htmlEncode(line1.value) =#_" class="ms-srch-video-intent ms-srch
                        _#= line1 =#_
                    </a>
                </h3>
<!--#
if (!mediaDuration.isNull)
{
_#-->
                    _#= mediaDuration =#_
```

Add the following code to that very same <div> tag:

onmouseover=" #= ctx.currentItem_ShowHoverPanelCallback =# "
onmouseout=" #= ctx.currentItem_HideHoverPanelCallback =# "

```
tem" onmouseover="_#= ctx.currentItem_ShowHoverPanelCallback =#_" onmouseout="_#= ctx.currentItem_HideHoverPanelCallback =#_">




h-video-results ms-srch-item-link ms-noWrap" id="_#= line1Id =#_">
```

Now add the following <div> after the first <div>:

<div id="_#= $htmlEncode(hoverId) =#_" class="ms-srch-hover-outerContainer"></div>

```
_#-->
<!--#_
              if (!Srch.U.n(ctx.CurrentItem.ParentTableReference) && ctx.CurrentItem.ParentTableReference.TotalRows > 1) {
_#-->
          <div id="_#= $htmlEncode(itemId) =#_" name="Item" class="ms-srch-people-intentItem" onmouseover="_#= ctx.currentIt
          <div id="_#= $htmlEncode(hoverId) =#_" class="ms-srch-hover-outerContainer"></div>
          <div id="VideoCard">
            <ul id="VideoCard">
              <li class="ms-srch-video-itemthumbnail">
              <a clicktype="Result" href="_#= titleLinkUrl =#_" id="_#= thumbnailPathId =#_">
                 _#= imageMarkup =#_
                  <div class="ms-srch-video-playbutton ms-srch-video-playbutton-result"><span></span></div>
              </a>
              </li>
              <li class="ms-srch-video-itemmain">
                <div id="_#= $htmlEncode(id + Srch.U.Ids.title) =#_" class="ms-srch-item-title">
                  <h3>
                     <a clicktype="Result" id="_#= $htmlEncode(id + Srch.U.Ids.titleLink) =#_" href="_#= titleLinkU
                        _#= Srch.U.trimTitle(title, maxTitleLengthInChars, termsToUse) =#_
                     </a>
                  </h3>
                </div>
              </li>
            </ul>
          </div>
          </div>
<!--#_
```

Save the changes to the template.

Navigate to your Search Center and perform a search that returns Video results:

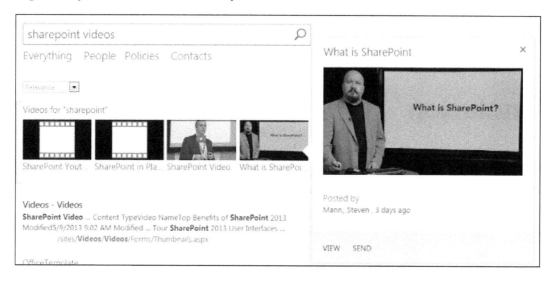

Hovering over the results shows the hover panel preview!!!

Conclusion

It is very easy to customize and enhance search results within SharePoint 2013. This guide focused on video based search results. I hope you found this information useful and easy to use. If there are any questions or problems, please send them to steve@stevethemanmann.com

Volume 4

How To Implement Remote Blob Storage in SharePoint 2013

STEVEN MANN

How To Implement Remote Blob Storage in SharePoint 2013

Copyright © 2013 by Steven Mann

Trademarks

Screenshots of Microsoft Products and Services

Warning and Disclaimer

Introduction

This guide outlines steps and configurations to implement Remote Blob Storage (RBS) in SharePoint 2013 using SQL Server 2012.

One of the advantages with the latest SharePoint versions and SQL Server versions is the ability to implement RBS using the FileStream Provider. This allows for documents and files that are larger than a specified amount of bytes (default 100KB) to be stored on a connected file system of the SQL Server box instead of inside the database itself. The overall advantage is keeping your content databases smaller and more manageable.

Reference links and source code are available on www.stevethemanmann.com:

Step 1: Enable File Stream on the SQL Server

On the SQL Server 2012 box, open SQL Server Configurations Manager.

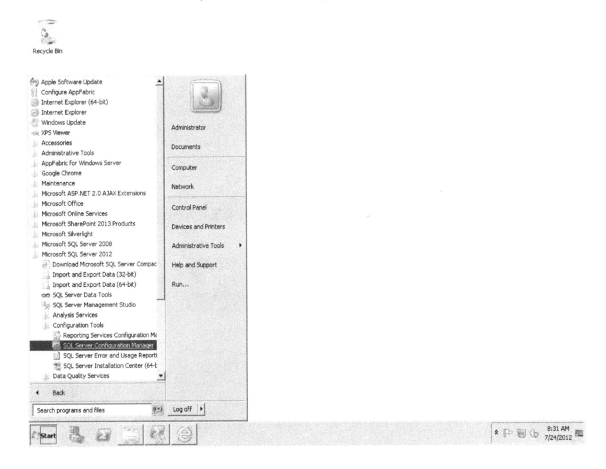

Select SQL Server Services from the left pane. Right-click on the SQL Server process in the right window and select Properties:

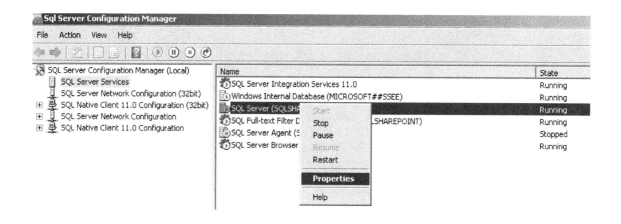

The SQL Server Properties dialog appears. Select the FILESTREAM tab and check all of the check boxes:

Click OK.

Start SQL Management Studio and open a new query window.

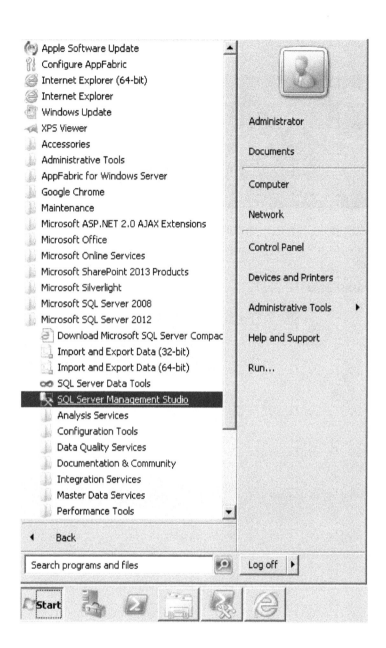

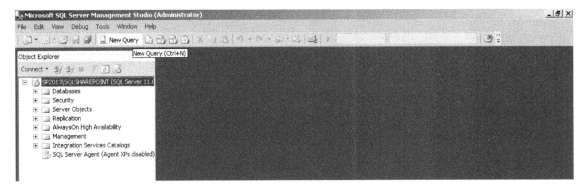

Execute the following two SQL Statements (on any database):

EXEC sp_configure filestream_access_level, 2

RECONFIGURE

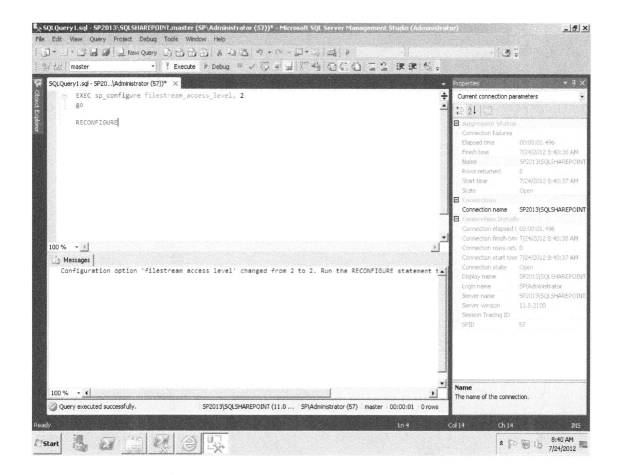

Using your content database open a new query:

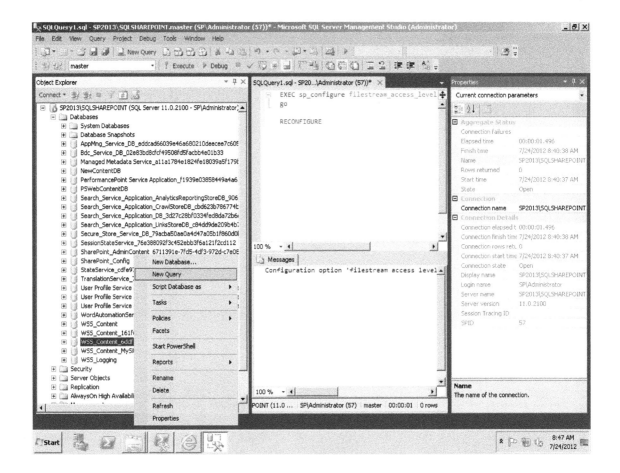

Create the master key using the following SQL:

```
if not exists (select * from sys.symmetric_keys where name
= N'##MS_DatabaseMasterKey##')
    create master key encryption by password = N'Admin Key Password !2#4'
```

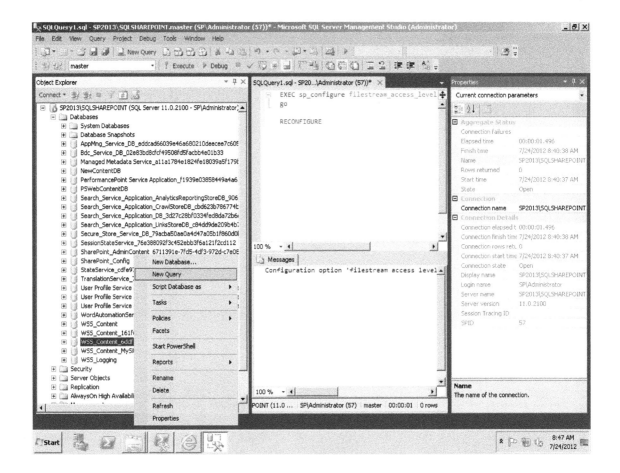

It is very important that the password is !2#4 - RBS will not work properly if this is not the password used.

Create a new filegroup for the RBS:

if not exists (select groupname from sysfilegroups where group-name=N'RBSFilestreamProvider')
    alter database [<your content database>]
    add filegroup RBSFilestreamProvider contains filestream

Add the "file" using the following SQL:

alter database [<your content database>]
add file (name = RBSFilestreamFile, filename= 'c:\SPBlobStorage')
    to filegroup RBSFilestreamProvider

SQLQuery3.sql - SP20...Administrator (131))* ✕ SQLQuery2.sql - SP20...\Administrator (52))*   SQLQuery1.sql - SP20...\Administrator (57))*

```sql
alter database [WSS_Content_6ddf1a64a957436589e0a80ad67f9301]
add file (name = RBSFilestreamFile,
        filename= 'C:\SPBlobStorage') to filegroup RBSFilestreamProvider
```

100 %

The "file" is a folder on a connected drive. It can be a local drive on the SQL Server or an attached iSCSI drive. The folder cannot exist already. Executing the SQL statement above automatically creates the folder specified on the drive specified.

Step 2: Install RBS on the DB and Web/Application Servers

The RBS bits need to be installed on the database server and on each Web server and Application server that exist in the SharePoint farm. The RBS bits are a separate installation as part of the SQL Server 2012 Feature Pack. You can access the feature pack for SQL Server 2012 here. (http://www.microsoft.com/en-us/download/details.aspx?id=29065)

Scroll down on the feature pack download page and locate the RBS download:

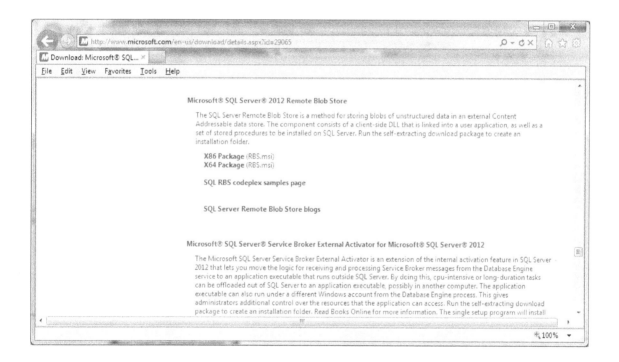

Download the appropriate package (hopefully x64) and save it in a central location.

For the first web server (or database server), create a new batch file, in the same location as you downloaded RBS.msi, using the following code (all on one line - no line breaks):

```
msiexec /qn /lvx* rbs_install_log.txt /i RBS.msi
```

TRUSTSERVERCERTIFICATE=true FILEGROUP=PRIMARY
DBNAME="<ContentDbName>"
DBINSTANCE="<DBInstanceName>"
FILESTREAMFILEGROUP=RBSFilestreamProvider
FILESTREAMSTORENAME=FileStreamStore

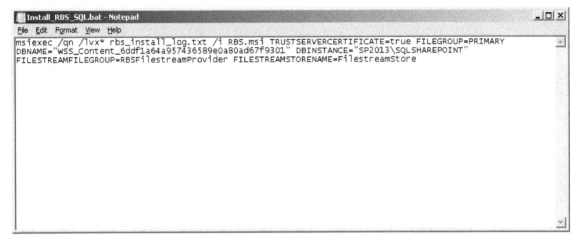

Open a Command Prompt and execute the first batch file:

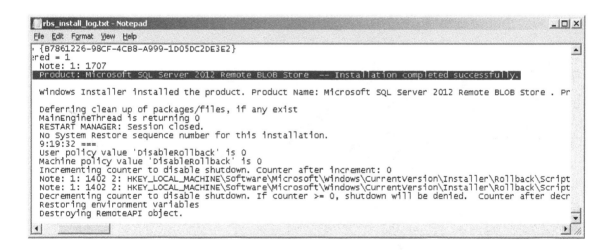

```
Y:\spblob>dir
 Volume in drive Y is Data
 Volume Serial Number is DEC1-B9DE

 Directory of Y:\spblob

07/24/2012  09:19 AM    <DIR>          .
07/24/2012  09:19 AM    <DIR>          ..
07/24/2012  09:18 AM               260 Install_RBS_SQL.bat
07/24/2012  09:06 AM         5,242,880 RBS.msi
               2 File(s)      5,243,140 bytes
               2 Dir(s)  37,604,794,368 bytes free

Y:\spblob>install_rbs_SQL

Y:\spblob>msiexec /qn /lvx* rbs_install_log.txt /i RBS.msi TRUSTSERVERCERTIFICAT
E=true FILEGROUP=PRIMARY DBNAME="WSS_Content_6ddf1a64a957436589e0a80ad67f9301" D
BINSTANCE="SP2013\SQLSHAREPOINT" FILESTREAMFILEGROUP=RBSFilestreamProvider FILES
TREAMSTORENAME=FilestreamStore

Y:\spblob>_
```

Verify success by reviewing the rbs_install_log.txt file that was generated in the same folder. The completion message is not the very last thing but it is towards the end of the log:

```
 {B7861226-98CF-4CB8-A999-1D05DC2DE3E2}
red = 1
 Note: 1: 1707
 Product: Microsoft SQL Server 2012 Remote BLOB Store  -- Installation completed successfully.

 Windows Installer installed the product. Product Name: Microsoft SQL Server 2012 Remote BLOB Store . Pr

 Deferring clean up of packages/files, if any exist
 MainEngineThread is returning 0
 RESTART MANAGER: Session closed.
 No System Restore sequence number for this installation.
 9:19:32 ===
 User policy value 'DisableRollback' is 0
 Machine policy value 'DisableRollback' is 0
 Incrementing counter to disable shutdown. Counter after increment: 0
 Note: 1: 1402 2: HKEY_LOCAL_MACHINE\Software\Microsoft\Windows\CurrentVersion\Installer\Rollback\Script
 Note: 1: 1402 2: HKEY_LOCAL_MACHINE\Software\Microsoft\Windows\CurrentVersion\Installer\Rollback\Script
 Decrementing counter to disable shutdown. If counter >= 0, shutdown will be denied.  Counter after decr
 Restoring environment variables
 Destroying RemoteAPI object.
```

On all of the other web servers and application servers, place the following code into a batch file (again no line breaks):

```
msiexec /qn /lvx* rbs_install_log.txt /i  RBS.msi DBNAME="ContentDbName"
DBINSTANCE="DBInstanceName"
ADDLOCAL="Client,Docs,Maintainer,ServerScript,FilestreamClient,FilestreamServer"
```

Open a Command Prompt and execute the second batch file on each web server and
application server:

Step 3: Enable RBS on the Content Database

To enable RBS on the content database, you must use PowerShell. Therefore, open up PowerShell or Notepad and create the following PowerShell Script:

```
$cdb = Get-SPContentDatabase -WebApplication "<Web Application Name>"
$rbss = $cdb.RemoteBlobStorageSettings
$rbss.Installed()
$rbss.Enable()
$rbss.SetActiveProviderName($rbss.GetProviderNames()[0])
$rbss
```

You may also add $rbss.MinimumBlobStorageSize=1048576 to increase the minimum file size that will be considered for RBS. The example number shows 1MB.

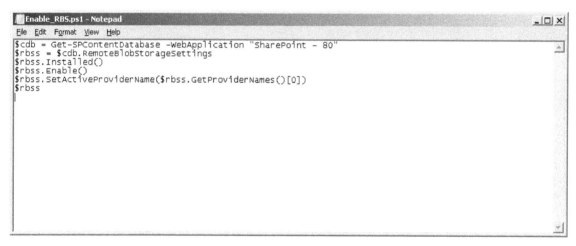

Save the script as a .ps1 file and then open the SharePoint 2013 Management Shell:

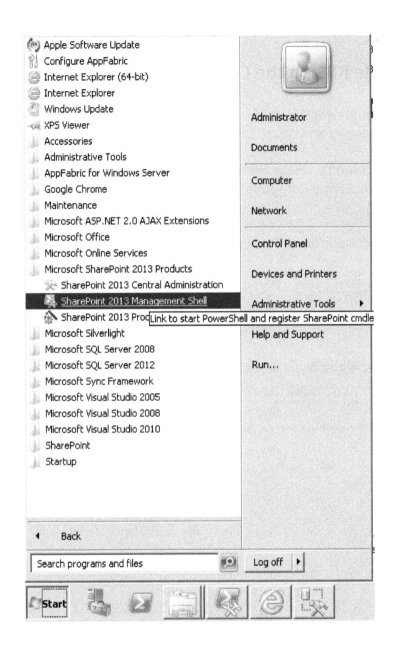

Execute the script:

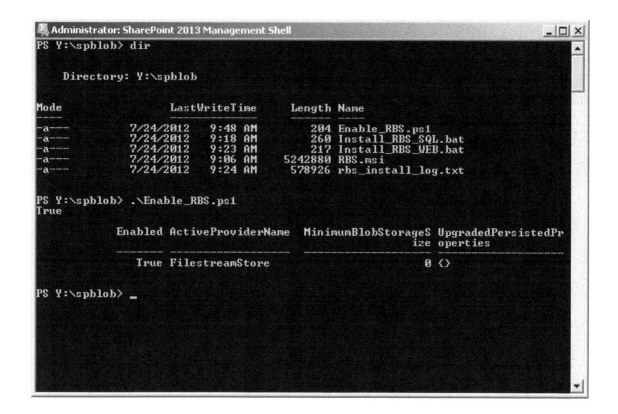

The first output is"True" which means RBS has been installed correctly. The second output displays the RemoteBlobStorageSettings object and shows that RBS is enabled and displays the name of the Active Provider (which should be the same name you used as the FILESTREAMSTORENAME in the RBS installation batch file.

Step 4: Test RBS

Now it's time to see this working in action! Navigate to your SharePoint site related to the content database you just configured. Open a document library:

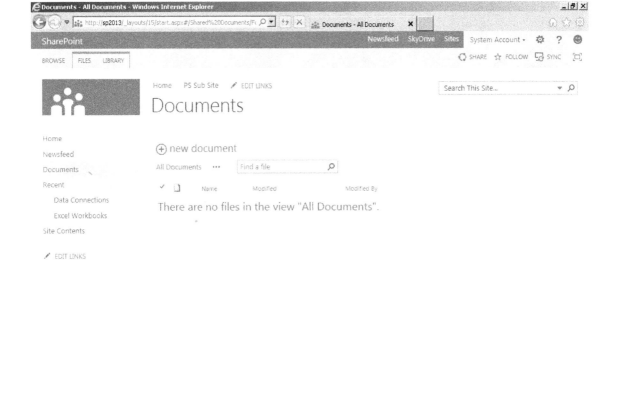

Upload a bunch of documents into the document library:

Documents

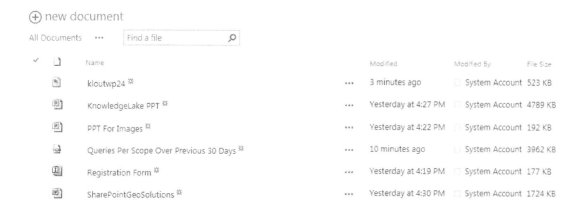

⊕ new document

All Documents ··· | Find a file | 🔍 |

✓	🗋	Name		Modified	Modified By	File Size
	📄	kloutwp24 ※	···	3 minutes ago	☐ System Account	523 KB
	📊	KnowledgeLake PPT ※	···	Yesterday at 4:27 PM	☐ System Account	4789 KB
	📊	PPT For Images ※	···	Yesterday at 4:22 PM	☐ System Account	192 KB
	📊	Queries Per Scope Over Previous 30 Days ※	···	10 minutes ago	☐ System Account	3962 KB
	📘	Registration Form ※	···	Yesterday at 4:19 PM	☐ System Account	177 KB
	📄	SharePointGeoSolutions ※	···	Yesterday at 4:30 PM	☐ System Account	1724 KB

Investigate the folders within the local file system blob storage location:

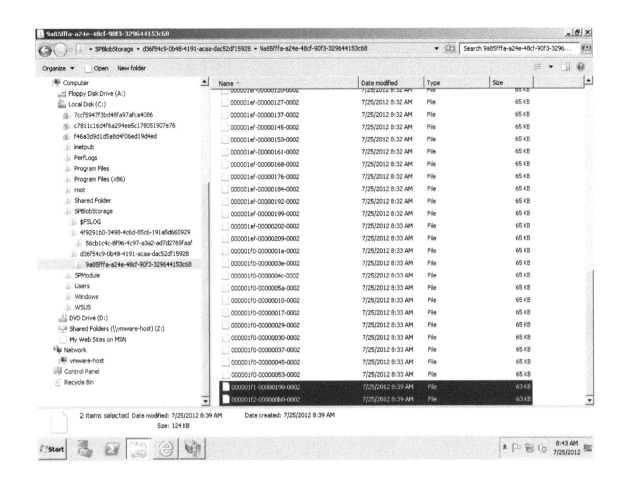

Files appear in small chunks. They will not be human readable.

Conclusion

This guide stepped you through the configurations to implement remote blob storage in SharePoint 2013 using SQL Server 2012. Enabling RBS with SharePoint 2013 is mostly configured on the SQL Server side and is possible because of the file stream provider. I hope you found the steps easy to follow and that this guide helped you implement RBS.

Volume 5

Finding Empty User Profile Properties in SharePoint 2013

STEVEN MANN

Finding Empty Profile Properties in SharePoint 2013

Copyright © 2013 by Steven Mann

Trademarks

Screenshots of Microsoft Products and Services

Warning and Disclaimer

Introduction

This guide steps through SharePoint PowerShell scripting that may be used to loop through your User Profile properties in SharePoint 2013 and identify missing information. User Profiles contain information about your users in SharePoint. There are many properties that may or may not be populated. With missing information, it may be hard to find someone or get the proper People search results.

While you may use the same code to find any user profile property, the example outlined in this guide finds all people that do not have their PictureURL populated, that is, the user does not have an associated picture in SharePoint.

Reference links and source code are available on www.stevethemanmann.com:

SteveMann's Path **s** SharePoint **Office**

Discussions on technology related to collaboration with SharePoint and InfoPath along with other cool and possibly geeky stuff.

Blog   Available Speaking Topics   Resource Links and Source Code

Step 1: Define Dynamic Variables

```
# Dynamic Settings
$mySiteUrl = "http://mysite.company.net"
$findProperty = "PictureUrl"
```

Step 2: Establish the Server Context

```
# Obtain Context based on site

$mySiteHostSite = Get-SPSite $mySiteUrl

$mySiteHostWeb = $mySiteHostSite.OpenWeb()

$context = Get-SPServiceContext $mySiteHostSite
```

Step 3: Instantiate a ProfileManager Object and Retrieve all of the SharePoint User Profiles

```
# Obtain Profiles from the Profile Manager
$profileManager = New-Object
        Microsoft.Office.Server.UserProfiles.UserProfileManager($context)

$AllProfiles = $profileManager.GetEnumerator()

$outputCollection = @()
```

Step 4: Loop through the profiles and retrieve the account name (for identification purposes) and the property you are interested in finding

```
# Loop through profiles and retrieve the desired property

foreach ($profile in $AllProfiles)

{

    $output = New-Object System.Object

    $output | Add-Member -type NoteProperty -Name AccountName -Value $profile["AccountName"].ToString()

    $output | Add-Member -type NoteProperty -Name $findProperty -Value $profile[$findProperty]

    $outputCollection += $output

}
```

Step 5: List out the collection items that do not have a value for the property (ie. null):

```
# List all Accounts that do not contain the property

$outputCollection | Where-Object {[bool]$_.($findProperty) -ne $true}
```

FULL SCRIPT

```
# Dynamic Settings

$mySiteUrl = "http://mysite.company.net"

$findProperty = "PictureUrl"


Write-Host "Beginning Processing--`n"


# Obtain Context based on site

$mySiteHostSite = Get-SPSite $mySiteUrl

$mySiteHostWeb = $mySiteHostSite.OpenWeb()

$context = Get-SPServiceContext $mySiteHostSite


# Obtain Profiles from the Profile Manager

$profileManager = New-Object Mi-
crosoft.Office.Server.UserProfiles.UserProfileManager($context)

$AllProfiles = $profileManager.GetEnumerator()

$outputCollection = @()
```

```powershell
# Loop through profiles and retrieve the desired property

foreach ($profile in $AllProfiles)

{

    $output = New-Object System.Object

    $output | Add-Member -type NoteProperty -Name Account-Name -Value $pro-
file["AccountName"].ToString()

    $output | Add-Member -type NoteProperty -Name $findProp-erty -Value $pro-
file[$findProperty]

    $outputCollection += $output

}


# List all Accounts that do not contain the property

$outputCollection | Where-Object {[bool]$_.($findProperty) -ne $true}
```

Conclusion

It is easy to use PowerShell to loop through User Profile Properties. The example in this guide identified all users who do not have a picture uploaded in their profile. You may use the full script to identify other user profile properties that may be missing information.